I0125787

Political Meritocracy and Populism

Offering the first in-depth analysis of the relationship between populism and political meritocracy, this book asks why states with meritocratic systems such as Singapore and China have not faced the populist challenge to the extent that liberal-democratic states have. Is political meritocracy immune to populism? Or does it fan its flames?

Exploring this puzzle, the authors argue that political meritocracies are simultaneously immune and susceptible to populism. The book maintains that political meritocracy's focus on the intellect, social skills, and most importantly virtue of political leaders can reduce the likelihood of populist actors rising to power; that meritocracy's promise of upward mobility for the masses can work against elitism; and that rule by the 'meritorious' can help avoid crises, diminishing the political opening for populism. However, it also shows that meritocracy does little to eliminate grievances around political, cultural, and social inequality, instead entrenching a hierarchy – an allegedly 'just' one. The book ultimately argues that the more established the system of political meritocracy becomes, the more it opens the door to populist resentment and revolt.

Pitched primarily to scholars and postgraduate students in political theory, comparative politics, Asian studies, and political sociology, this book fills an important scholarly gap.

Mark Chou is Associate Professor of Politics at the National School of Arts, Australian Catholic University, Melbourne, Australia.

Benjamin Moffitt is Senior Lecturer in Politics at the National School of Arts, Australian Catholic University, Melbourne, Australia.

Octavia Bryant is a Doctoral Candidate in Politics at the National School of Arts, Australian Catholic University, Melbourne, Australia.

Routledge Studies in Anti-Politics and Democratic Crisis
Series Editors: Jack Corbett
University of Southampton
and
Matt Wood
University of Sheffield

This book series aims to provide a forum for the discussion of topics and themes related to anti-politics, depoliticisation, and political crisis. We supposedly live in an anti-political age in which popular disaffection threatens to undermine the very foundations of democratic rule. From the rise of radical right wing populism through to public cynicism towards politicians, institutions and processes of government are being buffeted by unprecedented change that have in turn raised questions about the viability of seemingly foundational practices. The series is intentionally pluralistic in its geographic, methodological and disciplinary scope and seeks works that push forward debate and challenge taken-for-granted orthodoxies.

Refiguring Democracy
The Spanish Political Laboratory
Ramón A. Feenstra, Simon Tormey, Andreu Casero-Ripollés and John Keane

Re-thinking Contemporary Political Behaviour
The Difference that Agency Makes
Sadiya Akram

Political Meritocracy and Populism
Cure or Curse?
Mark Chou, Benjamin Moffitt, and Octavia Bryant

For a full list of available titles please visit
www.routledge.com/series/RSAPDC

Political Meritocracy and Populism

Cure or Curse?

Mark Chou,
Benjamin Moffitt,
and Octavia Bryant

R Routledge
Taylor & Francis Group

LONDON AND NEW YORK

First published 2020
by Routledge
2 Park Square, Milton Park, Abingdon, Oxon OX14 4RN

and by Routledge
605 Third Avenue, New York, NY 10017

First issued in paperback 2021

Routledge is an imprint of the Taylor & Francis Group, an informa business

Copyright © 2020 Mark Chou, Benjamin Moffitt, and Octavia Bryant

The right of Mark Chou, Benjamin Moffitt, and Octavia Bryant to be identified as authors of this work has been asserted by them in accordance with sections 77 and 78 of the Copyright, Designs and Patents Act 1988.

All rights reserved. No part of this book may be reprinted or reproduced or utilized in any form or by any electronic, mechanical, or other means, now known or hereafter invented, including photocopying and recording, or in any information storage or retrieval system, without permission in writing from the publishers.

Trademark notice: Product or corporate names may be trademarks or registered trademarks, and are used only for identification and explanation without intent to infringe.

Publisher's Note
The publisher has gone to great lengths to ensure the quality of this reprint but points out that some imperfections in the original copies may be apparent.

British Library Cataloguing-in-Publication Data
A catalogue record for this book is available from the British Library

Library of Congress Cataloging-in-Publication Data
Names: Chou, Mark (Political scientist), author. | Moffitt, Benjamin, 1985- author. | Bryant, Octavia, author.
Title: Political meritocracy and populism : cure or curse? / Mark Chou, Benjamin Moffitt, and Octavia Bryant.
Description: Abingdon, Oxon ; New York, NY : Routledge, 2020. | Includes bibliographical references and index.
Identifiers: LCCN 2019037633 (print) | LCCN 2019037634 (ebook) | ISBN 9780367271022 (hardback) | ISBN 9780429294846 (ebook)
Subjects: LCSH: Political culture. | Political culture–Singapore. | Political culture–China. | Populism. | Populism–Singapore. | Populism–China.
Classification: LCC JA75.7 ,C476 2020 (print) | LCC JA75.7 (ebook) | DDC 306.2–dc23
LC record available at https://lccn.loc.gov/2019037633
LC ebook record available at https://lccn.loc.gov/2019037634a

ISBN 13: 978-1-03-223908-8 (pbk)
ISBN 13: 978-0-367-27102-2 (hbk)

Typeset in Times New Roman
by Wearset Ltd, Boldon, Tyne and Wear

Contents

Acknowledgements

We wish to thank the series editors, Jack Corbett and Matt Wood for their interest in and support of this book from the outset. We also wish to thank the three anonymous reviewers whose comments on the project in its early stages helped us immensely. Thanks must also go to Claire Maloney at Routledge, and Claire Toal and Allie Hargreaves at Wearset for ably shepherding the book through the production and editing stages.

We thank our colleagues at the National School of Arts (Victoria) at the Australian Catholic University for their warm support and collegiality. Ben would also like to thank colleagues in the Political Theory seminar at his former institutional home, Uppsala University, Sweden, where an early version of this argument was presented, for their helpful feedback. Mark thanks Daniel Bell whose intellectual generosity and encouragement has helped to develop this work.

This research was partially supported by the Australian Government through the Australian Research Council's Discovery Early Career Researcher Award funding scheme (project DE190101127).

Finally, writing a book is always a collaborative process, with many people behind the scenes supporting and guiding the process. Mark would like to thank Rachel for coming into his life, and for her love. Ben would like to thank Ash and Will for their love, patience and support. Octavia would like to thank her partner, Jan van den Driesen for his encouragement and endless support, as well as her mum, Jan Bryant, whose intellectual guidance has been indispensable as she grows as a writer.

Introduction

Long-established democracies across Europe and North America are currently in the throes of a turbulent and seemingly unyielding populist revolt that has so far managed, with a surprising level of success, to drive a perceived political wedge between democracy and liberalism. From the Brexit vote and Donald Trump's election to the rising popularity of parties such as Italy's Five Star Movement, France's National Rally, Germany's Alternative for Germany, Spain's Podemos and the UK's Brexit Party, two things are clear. First, the rise of populism is not limited to one country or one hemisphere (Moffitt 2016). Second, liberal democracy in particular has proven to be an easy target for populist revolt (Pappas 2019; Galston 2018a). Though democracies in their various iterations have never been particularly good at spotting and stopping internal challengers (Keane 2009; Chou 2014), contemporary populists have demonstrated with undeniable clarity and efficacy how it is possible to exploit democratic procedures in order to disrupt deep-rooted liberal norms and patterns of party competition that, they argue, hinder the people from realizing their own democratic interests (Norris and Inglehart 2019; Galston 2018b). More so, in a time of political disruption and a growing sense of discontent and crisis, populists have proven to be highly effective at exposing the deficiencies and problems of liberal-democratic systems, whether exposing the 'democratic deficit' at the heart of elite projects like the European Union, the lack of actual choice offered to citizens in highly-curtailed party systems (Mair 2013), or the corruption, collusion, or falsities that are sometimes proffered in the name of liberal democracy.

Against this political backdrop – and the increasing sense that Western liberal democracies may not be equipped to stem the growing populist surge – scholars and commentators have begun asking whether other political systems from outside the West are able to offer potential insights, if not solutions, into how populism can be avoided in the first place, or at very least resisted. In particular, focus has often shifted to the East and

Southeast Asian context in this regard, with countries like Japan, Singapore, and even China topping the list of political contenders that have thus far managed to resist widespread populist uprisings. Here, popular commentary on these countries often claim that their political systems and societies are doing something different – and thus more effective when it comes to dealing with populism – than is the case in Western democracies. 'Even as a wave of right-wing populism is sweeping Europe, the United States, India, and parts of Southeast Asia', writes the former *The New York Review of Books* editor Ian Buruma (2018), 'Japan has so far appeared to be immune', pointing to its political culture and its protectionist economy as potential reasons for this. Similarly, commentators have noted how the city-state of Singapore has seemingly done 'away with populist pressures' by offering its citizens a different deal to what liberal-democratic countries offer theirs: against the public contestation and instability of liberal democracy, Singapore asks citizens to 'recede from public life in return for stable government, long-term thinking and economic growth' (Hendrie 2015, p. 174). Finally, in China of all places, there exists a broad view that even if the roots of a populist movement were to appear, the state would quickly suppress it. According to George Yeo (2017), Singapore's former Minister of Foreign Affairs, populism in China will be 'seen not in electoral terms but as an attempt to upset the political order'. For him, this is why any hints of populism will be 'curtailed at an early stage', something which we witnessed happen to movements like the Falun Gong as well as the political imprisonment of incipient populist Bo Xilai.

But are these Asian political systems as immune to the threat of populism as they appear – or as their political supporters would claim they are? Our aim in this book is to contribute to this line of questioning, but not with respect to all Asian countries or all Asian political systems, which we obviously acknowledge are not all uniform or of the same type. Rather, our objective is much more limited: to question whether one prominent Asian political system in particular can be considered immune to the threat of populism. That political system is political meritocracy.

In his influential yet controversial book, *The China Model: Political Meritocracy and the Limits of Democracy*, the political philosopher Daniel A. Bell argued that there are good reasons to believe that political meritocracy has the potential to act as a bulwark against populism. As he contended in the book's 2016 paperback preface, Western democracies differ from the political meritocracies that exist in countries like China and Singapore in the sense that democracies typically respond to troubled political and economic times by turning to 'angry and insular populism that only looks inside for solutions' whereas meritocracies tend to continuously 'innovate and learn from the rest of the political world' (Bell 2016,

p. xxvi). While populist politics certainly did thrive in China during the height of the Cultural Revolution, Bell claims that since China's opening up in the late 1970s, its embrace of meritocratic ideals and reforms in its political and bureaucratic circles have helped stem potential populist uprisings. Writing elsewhere, he put it more bluntly, saying that were China to do away with what he calls its 'vertical model of democratic meritocracy' to implement electoral democracy today, there would be little in the way of procedural checks and balances to stop citizens and elected officials from opting for short-term populist solutions over long-term policy proposals that may not always be politically popular (Bell 2017a, p. 154). In fact, the most likely outcome, as he put it, 'would be rule by a populist strongman backed by elements of the country's security and military forces' (Bell 2015) – a situation that sounds eerily familiar to watchers of populist regimes in the Philippines, Venezuela, and Hungary today. But luckily for China, Bell claimed that such a fate would be unlikely in the near future given the widespread public support for the practice of selecting and evaluating political leaders according to merit (Bell 2018).

He was, of course, right in one respect. Since the publication of *The China Model*, China's top leadership have steadfastly refused to embrace the prospect of implementing greater electoral democracy – especially at the central level. Yet what Bell may not have predicted when he wrote his book is that the Communist Party would not long after abolish term limits and effectively pave the way for President Xi Jinping to rule for life. Though a decision that obviously undermines the practice of political meritocracy – in the sense that a true political meritocracy cannot thrive when those who currently hold top leadership positions are empowered to hold them for life – Bell has remained adamant that the ideal that China's political system is guided by remains better suited to dealing with today's political challenges – populism included – than electoral democracies. As he put it in a 2018 book symposium response to critics of his work:

Electoral democracy may be appropriate for smaller countries or at lower levels of government of large countries; even if things go wrong – say, too much populism or small-minded gazing at the cost of neglecting long-term planning and concern for future generations and the rest of the world – it would not be the end of the world. But it may well be the end of the world if things go severely wrong at the top of big and powerful countries.

(Bell 2018, p. 112)

In other words, Bell seems to implicitly suggest that populism has not become more prominent in a country such as China because of the meritocratic measures put in place during the reform period. These measures aim to ensure that political officials and civil servants are selected and promoted based on their ability, virtue, and foresight rather than family lineage, personal connections, or political popularity alone. Even following the Communist Party's announcement that presidential and vice-presidential term limits would be abolished, his view is that the combination of the leaders' virtuous characteristics and the potential for anyone to become part of the ruling elite should remain as bulwarks against popular discontent, and thus populist uprisings against a corrupt elite.

Similarly, if we turn our focus to Singapore, the other established Asian political meritocracy, one oft-cited explanation for why the city-state has not succumbed to widespread populist incursions like its Southeast Asian neighbours in Thailand (under the Shinawatras) or the Philippines (under Duterte and Estrada) relates to its long-established system of political meritocracy (Tan 2008; Bellows 2009), which is explicitly 'structured to prevent the exercise of power by short-term-minded "populist" political leaders' (Bell 2016, p. 3). Despite holding regular elections, Singapore's political system is better characterized as a political meritocracy than electoral democracy. As Lee Kuan Yew (cited in Bell 2013, p. 3), the country's founding father, stated: 'Singapore is a society based on effort and merit, not wealth or privilege depending on birth. [The elite provides] the direction, planning and control of [state] power in the people's interests.' This foundational statement is now systematically entrenched within the city-state's civil service and political leadership, which recruits and assesses employees and candidates based on their performance and aptitude. As the Singaporean political scientist, Kenneth Paul Tan (2008, p. 11), has noted:

> In Singapore's national discourse, meritocracy is regularly and straightforwardly advanced as the only viable principle for organizing and allocating the nation's scarce resources to optimize economic performance and political leadership within conditions of vulnerability and resource scarcity. Not only has the term 'meritocracy' become enshrined and celebrated as a dominant cultural value in Singapore, it has also come to serve as a complex of ideological resources for justifying authoritarian government and its pro-capitalist orientations.

Understanding this state of affairs not only helps us to comprehend why the Chinese Communist Party has long looked to the city-state as a political model to replicate (Ortmann and Thompson 2014, 2016). It also offers initial insight into why populism's allure has largely failed to seduce either the country's citizens or leaders. As Tan (2017) reiterates, Singapore's 'rigorously meritocratic institutions', which have shown themselves capable of creating 'policies, even unpopular ones, that it deems to be in the long-term public interest', remain an important defence against the rise of populism. Furthermore, because the leadership of each country arguably continues to be driven by (at times, ruthless) pragmatism rather than strict ideology, the political culture of both China and Singapore tend to promote performance legitimacy over popular legitimacy alone, which again undercuts populist appeals to the people. 'Regarded as a crucial pillar in the [People Action Party's] mode of governance', scholars have thus maintained that 'the principle of meritocracy ensures that individuals are rewarded on the basis of ability and effort and not on the basis of race, class, or other ascriptive factors' (Wong and Huang 2010, pp. 531–532). Institutionally, the political culture is said to encourage 'thinking ahead, thinking again, and thinking across' (Ho 2018, p. 972). But there are limits to this 'cool-headed' approach: wary of appearing as cold, distant, and uncaring technocrats, Singapore's ruling elite have in recent years begun to push more 'compassionate and inclusive forms of meritocracy, focusing on skills and not academic qualifications alone, and implementing new programs that purport to advance continuous lifelong learning' (Tan 2017). As Michael Barr (2016, p. 5) notes, the point of all of this is to get a crucial message across: that Singapore's elite are not just 'highly competent', they are also 'exceptionally virtuous' as well. All told, these factors both work to prevent the likelihood that populist leaders would rise to power and undercut the potential for mass discontent that typically underpins populist uprisings.

This is the optimistic reading of the situation: the short-term, crisis-driven, anger-fuelled, people-centred politics of pessimism that has so defined both right- and left-wing populist discourse in Western democracies over the last several years has largely fallen flat in Asia's political meritocratic systems. Instead, it is the politics of optimism in terms of measured progress and economic growth – which once dominated American and European political outlooks – that now seems more at home in places like China and Singapore. There, as Singapore's Kishore Mahbubani (2016) has written, you will not find political leaders of the same ilk as a Trump, Le Pen, or Sanders enjoying anywhere near the support they receive in the West. Instead, he believes, you will only find the legacy of Lee Kuan Yew, and his famous political adage that favouring 'hard truths' is better than favouring 'politically convenient ones', living on (Mahbubani 2016, p. 28).

Yet if we dig somewhat deeper, the notion that political meritocracy is immune to populism starts to fall apart. While political meritocracies like China and Singapore may be *better equipped* than Western democracies in arresting the rise of incipient populism, by no means have populists been entirely absent from the meritocratic political landscape.

In China, for instance, the high-profile case of Bo Xilai – the disgraced former Chongqing party boss – offers perhaps the clearest illustration that populist tactics can still hold sway in a supposedly meritocratic system. Though Bo rose to political prominence as mayor of Dalian and governor of Liaoning, it was as Communist Party Secretary of Chongqing where his populist antics caused the greatest stir. What rocketed Bo to political stardom, and set him apart from other senior Communist Party of China (CPC) leaders at the time, was that he appeared less motivated by factional struggles within the party than appealing directly to the people and 'building a populist image' that might well have driven him to the very top of the CPC leadership structure had he not been ousted and jailed on charges of corruption (Womack 2017, p. 397; Stewart and Wasserstrom 2016; Richburg and Higgins 2012). As *The Economist* reported in 2011, 'Bo is a populist with an iron fist' (*The Economist* 2011). Tough on crime and critical of the country's embrace of unfettered capitalism, Bo tapped into the growing disillusionment of everyday citizens left behind by China's economic development with his attempts to revive the cult of Mao and encourage 'red' nostalgia (Buckley 2017). His 'Chongqing Model', which was a tacit rebuke of the 'Shenzhen Model' of capitalist economic development, advocated social justice and economic equality on behalf of the masses. One of the more noteworthy examples of this was a 2010 initiative to use profits generated by state-owned enterprises to build 800,000 subsidized apartments for the less well-off. For many Communist Party old guards and supporters of the New Left (Buckley 2017), Bo's short-lived but high-stakes political experiment amounted to a return to China's 'populist roots' that had been 'abandoned in the name of economic development' (Li 2011). In some ways, it was inevitable that Bo, who became regarded as perhaps 'the most perfect incarnation of contemporary Chinese populism' (Cabestan 2012, p. 73), would ruffle the feathers of the CPC's leadership. But even though the former Chongqing party boss is now long gone, languishing in Qincheng Prison, populism's presence remains. Despite being a very different man and political figure than Bo, Xi Jinping has, according to Devin Stewart and Jeffrey Wasserstrom (2016), similarly 'embraced a muscular nationalism not unlike those of Modi, Abe, and Duterte, and the domestic rival he vanquished'. Even outside the Communist Party's immediate sphere of influence, there is a growing brand of populist nationalism that has been fronting a challenge to China's political system and pushing for a more assertive Chinese approach in the South China Sea and with Western powers such as the United States (Li 2011).

While Singapore's smaller and more established meritocratic political system has not yet come close to producing a populist figure as prominent as Bo, significant anxiety about the potential threat of populism remains in the city-state, with Prime Minister Lee Hsien Loong recently warning that the country is not immune to divisive, populist politics (Huxley 2016). As Mr Lee explained, why populism has taken root in places like the United States is because 'the population feels anxious, feels unsettled, feels angry and doesn't feel that the existing political leadership and process is articulating or addressing those emotions' (Au Yong 2016). These are pressures, Mr Lee continued, that could also:

> build up in Singapore because, as a developed economy, we face some of the same challenges as they do. And if we are unable to address that, people will feel like there is no other avenue to have their concerns seen to, and their feelings spoken for.
>
> (Au Yong 2016)

What motivated the Prime Minister's statements were a series of worrying social and cultural developments within Singapore that had also been evident, albeit to a far greater extent, in Western countries which were facing the full brunt of populist ire, including escalating property prices, an influx of migrants, and over-burdened public infrastructure (*The Economist* 2015). Opposition parties, such as Singapore's Worker's Party, and disgruntled Singaporeans were quick to jump on these problems and cast blame on 'an increasingly self-regarding elite that seems too interested in staying in power and that citizens perceive as arrogant and unresponsive to their needs' (Tan 2016). While the PAP did take heed of the public's dissatisfaction, seeking to fashion a more 'compassionate' and responsive meritocracy to combat such anti-elite sentiment (Tan 2017; Wembridge 2015; Bell and Li 2013), Tan (2017) notes that 'ordinary Singaporeans continue to witness a rise in relative poverty, socio-economic inequalities, cost of living, and immigration'. What this means is that there may still come a time when these current problems could transform into the type of popular demands that are best championed by populist movements and parties (Laclau 2005).

There thus seems to be a critical disparity emerging between theory and practice: that is, between the *notion* that political meritocracies are somehow structured to prevent the emergence of populism and the *actual* populist developments taking shape in contemporary political meritocratic systems such as China and Singapore. This puzzling disparity also presents an important question that forms the focus of this book. This question is not 'why are political meritocracies immune to the threat of populism', but 'why are political meritocracies simultaneously immune *and* susceptible to populism'?

Through a critical engagement with the work of Daniel A. Bell in particular – who has been perhaps the leading contemporary advocate of both political meritocracy and its capacity to prevent the rise of populism – we first demonstrate in this book that there are three principal reasons why political meritocracies can theoretically be considered as relatively immune to populism, which we understand not as a distinct ideology or mode of organization, but rather as 'a political style that features an appeal to "the people" versus "the elite", "bad manners" and the "performance of crisis, breakdown or threat"' (Moffitt 2016, p. 45) that can be channelled or utilized by a variety of different political actors, whether leaders, parties, or movements. The first key reason has to do with the emphasis that political meritocracies place on the intellect, social skills, and most importantly virtue of political leaders, which helps reduce the likelihood of populist actors rising to political power (given that leaders in such systems should theoretically not be seen as illegitimate). The second reason we put forward is that the prospect of upward mobility for the masses in such political systems can help undercut the populist claim that society unfairly entrenches elitism and inequality. And third, we will demonstrate that rule by the meritorious can hypothetically increase a society's chance of steering clear of avoidable crises, which then diminishes the political opening for populism.

But while these reasons may help to make politics and society more just, we argue in response to the second part of our question that they do little to eliminate public grievances around political, cultural, and social inequality – frequently regarded as core drivers of populist success (Mudde 2007; Norris and Inglehart 2019). To the contrary, what the very ideal of meritocracy seeks to do is *entrench* a hierarchy (rather than a flatter power relation), albeit a more just one. In this respect, the objective of political meritocracy is the creation of a *justly unequal* society as opposed to an *unjustly unequal* one. Using the ideas of the twentieth-century sociologist Michael Young, we therefore conclude by claiming that the more established the system of political meritocracy becomes, the more it opens the door to populist resentment and revolt in the long run. To this end, even if China's and Singapore's meritocratic systems were fully developed, they would provide no ultimate guarantee against populism: the inequality entrenched in these systems still provides fruitful ground for populism to develop.

These insights are politically important given that they can feed into debates about how to practically deal with the challenges presented by populism across the globe at the current moment. At a time when liberal democracy seems to be under significant pressure it is critical to interrogate claims made about the efficacy of potential alternatives and 'solutions' for the populist challenge rather than taking them at face value. These insights also make a novel contribution to current scholarly and policy debates about populism's relationship to different political forms and systems. While there are substantial bodies of work on populism's relationship to liberal democracy (Mudde and Kaltwasser 2012; Müller 2016; Pappas 2019; Rummens 2017), fascism (Eatwell 2017; Finchelstein 2014, 2017), nationalism (Mudde 2007; De Cleen 2017) and technocracy (Bickerton and Invernizzi Accetti 2017; Caramani 2017; de la Torre 2013), surprisingly little systematic scholarship has been produced on the relationship between populism and political meritocracy. This is made even more surprising by the fact that meritocratic ideals now underpin the world's largest country and its next great superpower. In such a situation, such an analysis is not only timely, but is urgently needed.

That aside, there is also a potentially important correlation between the rise of political meritocracy in the East and democracy's demise in the West. As Bell (2016, p. 2) notes, that political meritocracy has become topical again is, at least, partly related to the internal political woes confronting many Western political systems – if all were well on the liberal-democratic scene, we likely would not even particularly be interested in the question of political meritocracy as an alternative system of governance. More specifically, he contends that as democratic voters begin to 'select populist leaders who advocate policies inimical to the long-term good of the country' during times of crisis, the case for improving Western democracies 'by incorporating more meritocratic institutions and practices' only becomes stronger (Bell 2016, p. 2). To this end, our aim is to further our understanding of whether and in what ways political meritocracy could in theory, potentially be a political system that may act as a bulwark against populism in the twenty-first century – and whether such protections actually create more problems than they purport to solve in the face of populism's rise.

However, before our analysis begins in full, two crucial points need to be acknowledged. First, it is important to note, as many of Bell's critics have done in relation to his claims about Chinese meritocracy in particular (Chan 2015; Nathan 2015; He 2016; Han 2017), that neither Singapore nor China can be regarded as *true* functioning political meritocracies. In both countries, the actual political system often undermines or actively subverts their respective meritocratic processes in order to ensure politically favourable outcomes. One of the clearest manifestations of this is the problem of ossification, a challenge that Bell has also acknowledged. As he writes: 'Given the wide distribution of talents in society, one would therefore expect that political leaders in meritocratic systems such as China and Singapore would come from diverse social backgrounds' (Bell 2016, p. 126). But the reality is often quite different. Indeed, in supposedly meritocratic China and Singapore, 'political hierarchies are increasingly composed of elites from a narrow social background' that set them apart from the people they represent (Bell 2016, p. 126). One of the biggest, ongoing indictments against China's political meritocracy is the distinct absence of women in top leadership positions. As Cheng Li (2017) demonstrates, women only make up the tiniest of minorities in the Communist Party's Politburo and Central Committee. Outside Beijing, not one of China's 31 provincial governments are led by women (Li 2017). Singapore's more meritocratic political system is similarly structured so that elite circles have become largely a closed and self-populating one. As Diane Mauzy and R.S. Milne's (2002) research has shown, the reality is that ordinary Singaporeans who manage to join the PAP will typically find it difficult, if not impossible, to rise through party ranks and be awarded a position of political power or prestige no matter how deserving they may be.

But ossification aside, there is an even more worrying recent development in China to flag: the Communist Party's 2018 decision to abolish presidential and vice-presidential term limits. Such a reform not only constitutes an enormous step in the wrong direction when it comes to China's democratic aspirations, it also threatens the country's already questionable meritocratic credentials. Empowering a ruler for life puts to the test the notion that the top of the political hierarchy will always be populated by the best, brightest, and most virtuous (Chou 2018). It also jeopardizes China's collective leadership and rotation of power, imperfect but important meritocratic mechanisms nonetheless put in place during the reform period to ensure the country's disastrous experiment with authoritarian populism never gets repeated. The most worrying aspect accompanying the return to personalistic rule under President Xi, according to the likes of Susan Shirk (2018), is the re-emergence of 'virtuocracy' that once thrived under Mao. Now, more than any point during the Reform period, 'getting ahead at school and work again depends at least in part on one's "redness"', according to Shirk (2018, p. 25). The power and influence that Xi, and his underlings, will likely amass over the coming years should worry both the champions of democracy *and* meritocracy in China.

In relation to this first point, we advance two claims. First, our analysis openly acknowledges that neither China nor Singapore are ideal types, but merely the most prominent empirical examples of political systems that are undergirded by political meritocratic aspirations in the contemporary political landscape. Both meritocracies currently suffer from a range of institutional, procedural, and ideological flaws that together expose the limits of their supposedly meritocratic credentials. China, in particular, now faces an uphill battle to ensure that patronage networks do not entirely undo the meritocratic reforms that have taken place over the previous few decades. Indeed, numerous reforms are needed in order to ensure these political systems continue to bridge the gap between the current reality and the meritocratic ideal (reforms that, at the time of writing, do not look as if they have any real chance of being implemented). Second and more importantly, we make the argument in this book that, even if countries like China and Singapore hypothetically managed to perfect their meritocratic political systems, they would still not be immune to the threat of populism. As noted earlier, this is because the very ideal of meritocracy is structured to entrench a 'justly unequal' hierarchy. In other words, it is not that inequality disappears or is sublimated into other forms as a meritocratic system becomes more 'perfected'. Rather, it is that the inequality within the system becomes perceived as more than just the random and distorted inequality of non-meritocratic systems. This lingering inequality – whether it is allegedly just or not – still presents a fruitful ground for populism. Indeed, as populists in Western democracies have clearly demonstrated, what has most angered the people is not necessarily the lack of justice in society, but the unequal hierarchy that separates them from the elite. This is why, as we will demonstrate, arguments that suggest a perfected meritocracy would somehow better prevent the rise of populism may actually prove false.

There is also a second point to note at the outset. It is clear that by focusing on China and Singapore in particular we are not examining competitive electoral systems. Both China and Singapore are police surveillance states that, to a greater or lesser extent, operate to stamp out mass political uprisings. But even though these two countries do not hold electoral contests in the mode that the most familiar cases of populism emerge from (or at least in the case of Singapore, not electoral contests that can be considered completely fair), it is not to say that populism will not arise in more authoritarian settings. In fact, there are good reasons to pay attention to how populism can emerge in less competitive settings. The burgeoning literature on hybrid regime types – often under the heading of competitive authoritarianism (Levitsky and Way 2010) or illiberal democracy (Mounk 2018) – have shown that such regimes can be very potent environments for populism, while Mudde and Rovira Kaltwasser (2017, p. 87) have argued that populism can actually have a positive liberalizing force in authoritarian regimes. The notion that populism can only emerge in 'truly' democratic systems is both Eurocentric and empirically wrong: while there of course needs to be some discursive or systematic 'opening' for talk of 'the people' versus 'the elite' to emerge, the fact of the matter is that populism has played an important and central role in hybrid regimes in Central and Eastern Europe, Africa, Latin America, and Asia – and to view it purely in its party form in established liberal-democratic party systems (as many scholars of populism in the Global North do) is limiting and stultifying. As such, it makes sense to turn our attention to how these less competitive regimes, based more on meritocratic ideals, can either help or hinder populism.

Our argument is set out over the four following chapters. Chapter 1, 'Political meritocracy and populism', lays out our definitions of our key concepts. We outline the core differences between electoral democracy and political meritocracy, and explain the primary theoretical tenets of political meritocracy as a political system. We examine Bell's claims about political merit being principally determined through three attributes – intellectual ability, social skills, and virtue – and consider how this separates political meritocracy from the closely-related concept of technocracy. We also set out our definition of populism as a distinct political style, and in doing so, consider how such a conceptualization of the concept is more useful for analysis of global cases – particularly those outside the liberal-democratic paradigm – than other prominent approaches to the phenomenon. Specifically, we consider how a stylistic definition of populism allows us to identify populism within settings that are not necessarily multi-party systems, and ask why populism is perceived to be a threat to democracy.

Chapter 2, 'Populism's cure?', considers the claim that political meritocracy provides a potential cure to the rise of populism. We consider the ways that political meritocracies such as China and Singapore guard against populism – namely considering the role of the leader in political meritocracies, the perception of fairness and justness in terms of procedures in political meritocracies, and the approach to crises in political meritocracies as opposed to democracies. We then consider how this plays out empirically in China and Singapore, and to challenge the 'populist cure' hypothesis, documenting the creeping presence of populist forces in supposedly meritocratic China and Singapore. In doing this, our objective is to emphasize the very real gap that currently exists between the ideal and reality of political meritocracy, and to address the argument that, as the gap closes, we should expect to see a corresponding decrease of populist politics in political meritocracies

Chapter 3, 'The populist teleology of meritocracy', considers the susceptibility of political meritocracies to populism. We do so by drawing on the work of the British sociologist Michael Young, whose story *The Rise of Meritocracy* (1958) provides an illustration of how the more that meritocratic ideals became entrenched into the political, economic, and cultural order, the more susceptible that order becomes to populist revolt. Given that political meritocracy does not seek to remove inequality – only make it more 'just' – we argue that the door remains open to populist discontent, as populists are often less motivated by eradicating injustice than inequality (whether perceived or real, economic, political, or cultural). This, we argue, is something that advocates of political meritocracy often fail to acknowledge or see.

In the Conclusion, we draw together the central arguments of the book and consider what the wider lessons are that can be drawn about the efficacy of political meritocracy against populism; the feasibility of political meritocracy; and the desirability of political meritocracy versus the challenges presented by populism. It more broadly locates such arguments within debates about how political orders across the globe can deal with the looming 'populist challenge' – and concludes by considering whether the 'cure' of political meritocracy for populism actually presents more problems than it purports to solve.

1 Political meritocracy and populism

According to Daniel A. Bell (2016, p. 2), China's long history with political meritocracy, which has its origins in the centuries-old imperial examination system whereby leaders were selected by means of examination and performance evaluations, was only halted at the start of the twentieth century, with the Qing dynasty's fall. What followed – the rise of Maoism and the disastrous Cultural Revolution that 'valued the political contributions of warriors, workers, and farmers over those of intellectuals and educators' – systematically undid any of the meritocratic ideals that the country had revered in generations past. When debates over political meritocracy finally re-emerged in the 1960s, it was not China, which was still under Mao's firm grip, but the tiny city-state of Singapore that best demonstrated how political institutions and procedures could be structured around an ideology that ensured leaders perceived as best equipped to make difficult decisions and take the long view were the ones selected for positions of power. It was only during the 1990s that the ideal of political meritocracy returned to China. Imperfect and piecemeal as its contemporary experimentation has been, it is clear that the country now aspires to establish a more comprehensive system for selecting and promoting political leaders based on their merits instead of their popularity or power alone.

While Bell argues that the discourse on political meritocracy failed to achieve greater international appeal due to it never having been presented as a universal ideal in the same way that democracy has been, it is his implication that political meritocracy is structured to prevent the rise of populism that interests us here. Indeed, what lies implicit in Bell's historical overview of this ideal is a simple, but important claim: where political meritocracies have thrived, populism has not. The aim of this book is to examine this claim, both in theory and through empirical examples.

However, in order to scrutinize how political meritocracy supposedly acts as a bulwark against populist forces, we need to first define political meritocracy and populism before examining how the former might potentially prevent the rise of the latter. In this chapter, we differentiate political meritocracy from a purely technocratic style of governance in the sense that a political meritocratic system is not only underpinned by expertise and intellectual ability, but more importantly by attributes such as virtue and social skills as well. In this way, political leaders will need to demonstrate more than their technical expertise and capacity for rational decision-making. They will have to exhibit virtue along with a respect for common people. As for populism, we outline the three central approaches to the phenomenon in the academic literature – the ideational approach, the strategic approach, and the discursive-performative approach – and consider their suitability and applicability to understanding populism in political meritocracies such as China and Singapore. We ultimately argue that the discursive-performative approach is most useful for our purposes, and draw on Moffitt's (2016) definition within this approach of populism as a political style as a basis for our argument.

Following this, we go on to demonstrate the ways in which political meritocracy might help thwart the forces of populism. This analysis fills an important gap because, despite the various claims that have been made about political meritocracy's capacity to weather populism's challenge, very little systematic scholarship has been produced about why or how this is the case. Yet this is an essential task if such claims are to be methodically validated and scrutinized.

Defining political meritocracy

When it comes to the idea of meritocracy today, especially in the West, the likelihood that such a notion will be defined in strictly political terms is slim. Indeed, according to many Western accounts, the most common understanding of meritocracy is as an economic ideology and system that distributes wealth and resources on the basis of individual ability and effort rather than class and connections (Frank 2016; Saunders 2006; Lister 2006; Bell 1972). It is the idea that one's pedigree should present no permanent barrier to economic and social mobility. Unlike in times past, privilege and power should therefore not be determined by birth but by achievement. Given this, economic meritocracy is now sometimes considered as a harbinger of order and equality in capitalist economies (Lipsey 2014). It is considered a social positive that is both commensurate with the ideals espoused by neoliberal capitalism and liberal democracy. As Chang-Hee Kim and Yong-Beom Choi (2017, p. 112) have made clear, this economic variant of meritocracy 'has increasingly been recognized as a positive system in Western societies, and the ideology has been tightly coupled with the notions of capitalism and egalitarian values, which are fundamental to the concept of the "American Dream"'.

But while the idea of economic meritocracy is now long-established and entrenched in many Western democracies, the notion that political leaders should be selected and promoted not by popular vote but by their political abilities and efforts tends to be a practice found primarily in a select number of non-democratic regimes. In other words, whereas the idea of economic meritocracy has become widely associated with Western political and economic ideals, the idea of political meritocracy remains a largely puzzling – if not completely distasteful – notion to many in the democratic West. But what does the idea of political meritocracy entail at its core? Simply put, the central characteristic of political meritocracy is that the principle of merit stands above all else in governing how politics, political actors, and political institutions are selected, structured, and promoted (Tan 2008). In such political systems, merit – and not popularity – is what confers political authority and thus legitimacy (Bell 1972). Though the principle of merit can be broadly understood as 'IQ plus effort' (Young 1958), the notion of political meritocracy seeks to ensure government is comprised of those who are sufficiently qualified and experienced based on meritocratic considerations such as intellect, credentials, education, virtue, and past performance (Hui and Gore 2017). This may sound relatively straightforward an endeavour. Yet in practice, how merit is defined, in what context, and by whom are highly contested matters (Zeng 2013). For instance, while merit can simply entail 'employing the "expert and experienced"' in some political positions, it will require those who can 'competently manage the systemic links of our integrated societies' and 'yield "knowledge-based choices" on tough issues' in other positions (Gardels 2013, p. 6). In political meritocracies where periodic elections are held, the question of merit and which political ruler is deemed to possess it is also (at least partly) given over to the will of the people, which can make pinpointing the attributes of merit even more difficult (Tan 2008). This is why Bell (2013, p. 13) notes that it is important, when thinking about political meritocracy, to question 'which abilities matter? Which virtues matter? How do we measure politically relevant abilities and virtues? And how does context shape the need for different sorts of rulers?'

Political meritocracy is an idea with both Western and Eastern heritages and meanings. It would probably not surprise many to learn that philosophers such as Plato believed that leadership should be reserved for those with the 'capacity to grasp the eternal and immutable' rather than 'the mob' (Plato 2007, p. 204; Wolff 2006, p. 67). This is essentially a meritocratic argument. Today, as Tan (2008, p. 13) has demonstrated, there are clear parallels between how Singapore's PAP is structured – with its upper

echelon comprised of party's Central Executive Committee, cabinet minis-
ters, and parliamentarians – and the philosopher-kings of Plato's *Republic*
and the nocturnal council of his *Laws*. Yet where the idea truly flourished
in practice was arguably not in the West, but through the ideas of Confucius and Imperial China's civil service examination system (*Keju*), which
existed from the Warring States Period (453–221 BC) to the early twentieth-
century. With its origins in Confucianism and Daoism during the fifth and
six centuries BC, it was later taken up and developed by the Legalists (Liu
2016). Replacing the pedigree-oriented system of the Spring and Autumn
period (770–453 BC), the examination system, first established in 608 BC
during the Sui Dynasty, put a premium on 'evaluating the worthy' in determining the suitability of individuals to serve the Emperor and hold positions of political significance (Bell 2016, p. 65). As Confucius (cited in
Shin 2013, p. 264) once put it, 'If good men were put in charge of governing for a hundred years, they would be able to overcome violence and dis-
pense with killing altogether.' So firm was the ancient Chinese
philosopher's conviction in this principle that he even insisted the sons of
kings should be demoted to the standing of common people if they fail to
demonstrate the required merits for ruling – and vice versa. Yet like Plato,
Confucius did not believe that governance should be left to the masses;
rather, it should be reserved for *junzi* or exemplary people skilled in the
Way (ethical living) (Shin 2013, p. 266).

Despite the vast differences and contrasting schools of thought that
emerged with respect to Imperial China's examination system, it is
widely regarded as the world's first standardized tests for assessing
potential candidates' merits for taking political office (Bell 2016, p. 82).
As the system became more rigorous and established, it thus challenged
previous practices of selection based on sex, ethnicity, stock, and connections. And though social mobility was never its main purpose, the
examination system did undermine the political domination of established aristocratic families. Another consequence of the examination
system was providing implicit checks on the sovereign's incompetence
and abuse of power. For example, a proposal put forward by Xunzi
advocated that the monarch should increasingly delegate routine matters
to aides who were meritocratically selected to carry out such tasks (Bell
2016, p. 86) – a piece of advice that might prove prescient for the current
rule of Xi. Overall, the entire examination system was responsible for
instituting an ideal of political merit underpinned by qualities such as
'learning, administrative skills, moral quality, righteousness, uprightness
and conscientiousness' (Chu 1957, p. 237).

When it comes to its exact meaning, Zhang Yongle (2018) argues that
the term meritocracy also has different connotations in English compared

to Mandarin. In the former, according to the Peking University legal scholar, merit merely implies a 'praiseworthy quality' that is underpinned by one's talent and achievement (Zhang 2018, p. 52). It is a social good that is grounded in individual attributes and toil. But when it comes to Mandarin, meritocracy is comprised of the:

> characters for 'ability' [*neng* 能] and 'virtue' [*xian* 賢]. Ability is usually defined in terms of a functional relationship, but virtue can transcend practicality and efficiency, even coming to represent a political community or a civilization's idealization of the model human.
>
> (Zhang 2018, p. 52)

Why this is politically significant is that the Chinese understanding of meritocracy exceeds ability, which is typically an individual attribute, to encompass virtue, which encapsulates the highest aspirations of an entire community and even a civilization. Given this, the meritorious were not simply hard-working technocratic experts who could make hard decisions and take the long view. They were, in the Confucian understanding, *junzi* who would be virtuous elites driven by the collective good.

Many of these ideals and meanings have filtered into, and now underpin albeit in highly imperfect form, actual political meritocracies today. Take modern-day China for instance. Even with its many political problems, China's political bureaucracy now ranks among the most competitive in the world. Yet it is not competitive in the democratic, electoral sense. Rather, since the Reform era aspiring governmental officials have been required to pass a gauntlet of public service examinations and to demonstrate their achievements and worthiness not simply at the beginning of their careers but throughout. Particularly since the turn of the century, Chinese leaders have been primarily selected and promoted based on academic, technocratic, or virtue-based merit (Osnos 2015). Though some Western scholars have labelled him a scholarly apologist for the Chinese Communist Party (Chan 2015), the noted Chinese intellectual Zhang Weiwei (2012) firmly believes that the CPC 'may arguably be one of the world's most meritocratic institutions' where 'performance in poverty eradication, job creation, local economic and social development, and, increasingly, cleaner environment are key factors in the promotion of local officials'. Indeed, it is hard to deny that many at the top of the CPC leadership 'have served at least twice as party secretary of a Chinese province or at similar managerial positions', some of which are 'on average the size of four to five European states' (Zhang 2012). While sceptical observers might want to simply discard Zhang's statement in its entirety, a more nuanced take may be to question whether it is meritocratic considerations alone that drive the CPC's decisions to select and promote the candidates that it does, or whether such promotions are ultimately due to Party allegiance or family connections. But Zhang's boosterism aside, there is now sufficient academic scholarship on Chinese public administration, human resource management, and civil service to suggest that the ideal of meritocracy – though far from perfect in practice – has increasingly become institutionalized throughout the country's bureaucratic system (Burns and Wang 2010; Chan 2010).

But the question still remains: what specifically amounts to, or constitutes, political meritocracy today as understood, if not always practiced in its entirety, in contexts such as China and Singapore? To answer this question, we draw primarily from the scholarship of Bell, who has most systematically set out the key tenets of political meritocracy. Writing primarily about China – and the meritocratic model Singapore offers to the fledgling world power (Ortmann and Thompson 2016; Wong and Huang 2010) – Bell's argument is that political merit is today principally determined through a set of three key attributes. These are the attributes that aspiring civil servants and public officials must demonstrate when seeking selection or promotion for political posts.

The first of these attributes is a civil servant's or political leader's *intellectual ability*. Indeed, what is often said to distinguish a meritocracy from a democracy at the broadest level is that the intellect and expertise of political leaders will be valued to a far greater extent in the former compared to the latter. The key justification for this is simple. In recognition of the rather uncontroversial reality that modern-day governance is becoming increasingly complex, polycentric, technical, fast-paced, and globalized, political leaders and policy makers have to possess competency across a range of disciplines and pursuits, including economics, science, and international relations at the very least (Bell 2016, pp. 79–80). In China, aspiring government officials and political leaders must endure a battery of public service examinations that test their knowledge of CPC policies and issues facing China, and perform well in each post and level of government before being moved up the chain of command (Zhang 2012). Beginning with the 1993 *Provisional Regulations on State Civil Servants*, explicit meritocratic measures were established for recruitment, performance appraisal, recognition and award, and finally promotion (Zhang 2015). These practices were further cemented with the *Civil Servant Law of the PRC*, which came into effect in 2006, which has ensured cadres are appointed only after successfully progressing through six selection stages: democratic nomination, democratic assessment, public opinion poll, analysis of actual achievements, interviews, and comprehensive deliberation (Hui and Gore 2017, p. 5). With often thousands of prospective candidates competing for a single government post, political aspirants thus understand that to succeed means improving their knowledge and performance (Bell and Li 2013). Similarly, Singapore's meritocratic system places a premium on political candidates' academic credentials and job accomplishments; before the PAP allows candidates to run for office or enter the public sector, they must prove themselves capable and worthy (Bellows 2009, p. 27). Once there, as Michael Barr (2016, p. 7) observes, 'the ruling elite creams off those it considers best suited to senior leadership positions in the public sector or in politics'. Though citizens do have the ability to choose which representatives they ultimately want through the country's periodic elections, the reality is that their choice is for all intents and purposes limited to a pool of candidates predetermined by the PAP to be intellectually superior (Ortmann and Thompson 2014, p. 447). What this means is that there is an intensely competitive intra-party process to identify and nurture the most intellectually capable candidates before Singaporeans even have the opportunity to appraise them.

Intrinsic to this attribute is the equally important considerations of experience and expertise. Unlike elected officials in the West, who can come to office with very little previous relevant political or professional experience, civil servants and leaders in political meritocracies typically have to rise through the ranks, a long and arduous process whereby they have to demonstrate that they have gained the necessary experience and expertise for promotion (*The Economist* 2015). Given this, even when new leaders take the helm, rarely will they be as politically inexperienced as a Donald Trump or even a Barack Obama when they first assumed the presidency in the United States. Emphasizing intellect, experience, and leaders' capacity to engage in informed decision-making can be a stark contrast from Western democracies such as the US, where research frequently underscores how little elected representatives know about politics – which, in some instances, is precisely what makes them so appealing to the masses (Chou 2017; Brennan 2016; Achen and Bartels 2016; Somin 2013). Indeed, as the American political scientist Tom Nichols (2017) recently demonstrated in his book, *The Death of Expertise*, Americans now openly celebrate ignorance, especially when it comes to matters of politics and public policy. For Nichols (2017, p. 210), Trump's electoral victory in 2016 was 'one of the most recent – and one of the loudest – trumpets sounding the impending death of expertise'.

Bell's second attribute of political merit is *social skills*. Recalling a 2012 discussion with Li Yuanchao, who was then Minister of the Organization Department of the CPC Central Committee, Bell (2016, p. 170) notes that as important as intellectual ability is, political merit must also take into account a leader's capacity to engage with those under their rule.

'At the higher levels [of government]', he writes, paraphrasing Li, 'more emphasis is placed on rationality since cadres need to take multiple factors into account and decision making involves a much broader area of governance', but this does not mean that 'concern for the people' and 'a practical attitude' become irrelevant. In other words, book smarts on their own are insufficient for good leadership – IQ must be supplemented with EQ or emotional intelligence. Unfortunately, given the importance that the CPC has placed on intellectual merit over the years, political leaders have often taken the mould of distant and stony-faced technocrats who are neither capable of understanding nor relating to the common citizen. Especially when leaders are meritocratically selected by the CPC, and not chosen through popular elections, appealing to everyday people can become a second or third order consideration. In this regard, democratically-elected politicians have a clear advantage given their need to sustain their popular legitimacy by connecting with voters both on the campaign trail and while in office. But even so, contemporary political meritocracies are now beginning to appreciate the importance of nurturing social abilities in their would-be leaders.

Here, Bell looks specifically to recent PAP reforms in Singapore as examples. Whereas Singaporean leaders of generations' past were selected solely off their superior performance and knowledge of disciplines such as economics and engineering – expertise needed to build the city-state and lift its citizens out of poverty – the emphasis has gradually shifted to 'communicative talent and emotional intelligence' to ensure they do not alienate vast populations, especially young people who are energized by charismatic and socially-savvy politicians (Bell 2016, p. 90). Specifically, the PAP has gone about implementing a number of reforms in an effort to change its image as a 'macho-meritocracy' (Vogel 1989, p. 1053). A significant reform in this respect is its increasing efforts to recruit candidates from all sectors of society. The PAP seeks legitimacy not only by choosing the best, but by demonstrating that 'the "best" can be drawn from any social background', writes Tan (2008, p. 13). Another example, which followed in the aftermath of the poor results of the 2011 election, is the PAP's introduction of more social initiatives to engage and involve the community (Ortmann and Thompson 2016, p. 45). Leaders now actively promote grassroots organizations, such as the PAP Community Foundation, the People's Association, and Meet-the-People sessions for members of parliament in kindergartens, supermarkets, and through activities like cooking and sewing classes (Ortmann and Thompson 2014, p. 44). They also use social media – the PAP even has its own app – to connect with citizens and ensure citizens are connected to government.

The final attribute of political merit, according to Bell, is *virtue*. A good political leader and system is a virtuous one. History has known many intellectually-superior and socially-savvy leaders who turned out to be tyrants, sociopaths, and mass murderers. This is why any meritocracy that fails to include virtue is incomplete. For Confucius, virtue could encompass several qualities, including sincerity, seeking advice from the governed, respect, and caring for common people. More importantly, as Confucius (cited in Shin 2013, p. 265) writes in *The Analects*: 'If a person has talents as fine as the Duke of Zhou, but is arrogant and mean-spirited, the other qualities are not worth notice.' Without virtue, in other words, there is no authority to rule. No matter how smart or relatable a leader is, without virtue there will likely be a meritocratic glass ceiling that halts their rise to the top of the political hierarchy. This is the important point of difference that separates meritocracy from technocracy, argues Doh Chull Shin (2013, p. 265).

But while virtue is perhaps easy to define in the abstract, the tricky question is: how it should be articulated and assessed in political practice? Though Bell (2016, pp. 103–104) acknowledges that the practicality of assessing virtue can be inherently problematic and contested, he advocates that a good if basic measure would be to prohibit candidates with criminal records for serious crimes such as murder, rape, or even corruption to take examinations for entry into public office. Added to this should be a more positive measure: a good gauge for virtue may simply be whether politicians are willing to jettison self-interest for the good of the people. In this sense, virtuous politics 'means that, at a minimum, the ruler must serve the interests of the ruled, and not the ruler himself' (Bell 2017b). If they are willing, for example, to suffer for the greater good by doing volunteer work or helping poor communities over long periods of time, then there is a case to be made about the politician's virtue (Bell 2016, p. 104). To aid the spread of virtue in society, Bell (2018b) has also argued for more Confucian moral education. Somewhat like civic education in the West, Confucian moral education is now part of the formal education system in Chinese schools and used in the training of public officials.

At the core of this push to insert virtue into politics is the need to avoid what the American philosopher Michael Sandel (2017) has called 'meritocratic hubris' or the tendency for those who have risen to the top 'to look down upon the less fortunate'. When this happens over long periods, leaders can become detached from their own people and forget they are there to serve the public interest. Singapore Prime Minister Loong underscored this point when he stated: 'If you are successful, don't say it's just because of yourself. It's because of the system, it's because many people have helped you succeed. So you owe them something, you owe the system something, you owe Singapore something.' All this explains why Bell believes the problem of corruption is so significant for political meritocracies. A virtuous politician and political system should be fundamentally corruption-free. Yet at least in China's case, systemic corruption has been part and parcel of its political meritocracy (Bell 2017a, 2015). Understanding this – and that the legitimacy of China's guardianship discourse will be undermined if those who wield power continue to benefit from those who do not – President's Xi's anti-corruption campaign is thus one policy, problematic as it has been in practice, which Bell sees as fundamental to ensuring the future of meritocratic governance in China. Related to this has been Bell's (2013, p. 22) call to make a clearer distinction 'between the good of the political community and the good of the Chinese Communist Party' – a truly meritocratic system must put the good of the whole country and all those affected by government policies ahead of the party's fortunes.

Together, these three attributes – intellectual ability, social skills, and virtue – form the basis of Bell's model of contemporary political meritocracy. Of course, there is much to this model, as Bell himself has acknowledged, that currently remains nothing more than a political aspiration. In other words, there is a clear gap between the ideal presented through his model and the reality of what is actually taking place in political systems like China. But that does not mean we should throw the baby out with the bathwater. Though how political meritocracy is presently practiced remains far from perfect, the ideal of political meritocracy remains a political aspiration worth fighting for. As Bell (2018b, p. 901) writes, today:

> the problem is the gap between the ideal and the reality – worsening in some respects (such as the recent abolishment of term limits) and improving in others (such as the recent efforts to combat corruption) – rather than the ideal itself.

These are points which we return to in the following chapter.

Defining populism

What about populism? While meritocracy and more specifically, political meritocracy may be concepts that attract a large degree of debate, this pales in comparison to the arguments around the concept of populism. While these debates about how to define populism have been taking place in the fields of political science and political theory for a long time, they have tipped over into public view in recent years: in the wake of the success of political leaders, parties and movements that have been commonly interpreted as populist, a slew of major media publications have published pieces asking the question 'What is Populism?' This has been most pronounced following the 2016 twin shocks of Donald Trump winning the US presidential election and the success of the Leave campaign in the Brexit referendum in the UK, with populism arguably becoming the most hyped political phenomenon of the twenty-first century. This led *Cambridge Dictionary* to name populism its 'Word of the Year' in 2017, noting its importance as 'a phenomenon that's both truly local and truly global, as populations and their leaders across the world wrestle with issues of immigration and trade, resurgent nationalism, and economic discontent' (Cambridge Dictionary 2017).

These debates about the meaning of populism go back decades. Indeed, one of the early foundational texts in the study of populism was Ionescu and Gellner's 1969 edited collection *Populism and its National Characteristics*, which drew together papers from a conference held two years earlier at the London School of Economics by the name of 'To Define Populism'. To put it bluntly (and perhaps obviously), the conference did not achieve its goal of one parsimonious and authoritative definition – rather, its participants variously described populism as an ideology, a type of political movement, and a 'political syndrome' amongst other possibilities, with the concept being applied to a truly dizzying array of cases. As one of the contributors to the volume put it at the time, 'to each his own definition of populism, according to the academic axe he grinds' (Wiles 1969, p. 166) – a worthy description not only of the academic debates of the time, but of the debates around the concept that would follow over the following 50 years.

Thankfully, in the ensuing decades, a great deal of progress has been made in terms of the conceptual development and understanding of populism, not only in terms of what it 'is' as a concept, but also in terms of considering the types of phenomenon it applies to, its normative underpinnings, its effects on democracy, and how it tends to manifest in different parts of the world. Rather than being an impenetrable and unwieldy literature, work on populism has arguably settled into three broad conceptual approaches: the ideational approach, which views populism as an ideology, worldview, or particular set of attitudes; the strategic approach, which sees populism as a strategy or mode of organization used by political leaders; and the discursive-performative approach, which sees populism as a mode of speaking, acting, or constructing political subjects. Each of these main approaches have important theoretical and methodological differences, particularly when it comes to determining how we identify a case of populism. In this section, we outline the basics of each of these approaches, before outlining why we consider the discursive-performative approach most suitable for exploring the relationship between populism and political meritocracy in China and Singapore.

First, we have the ideational approach to populism. This approach is arguably the most popular, well-known, and widely used definition of populism in the contemporary literature on the topic. As noted, this approach tends to view populism as an ideology, a set of ideas, a way of seeing the world, or as a set of distinct attitudes – in other words, it takes the '-ism' part of populism seriously, putting it alongside other 'isms' understood to be ideologies or worldviews like socialism, liberalism, libertarianism, environmentalism, and so on. The main definition used under this approach is that of Cas Mudde, who sees populism as 'a thin-centered ideology that considers society to be ultimately separated into two homogeneous and antagonistic camps, "the pure people" versus "the corrupt elite", and which argues that politics should be an expression of the *volonté générale* (general will) of the people' (Mudde 2004, p. 543). By 'thin' ideology – a term not only used by Mudde, but picked up and developed by Stanley (2008), Albertazzi and McDonnell (2008), and Rooduijn (2014) – it is understood that populism does not 'stand alone' as a 'full' ideology, but rather is always present in mixed iterations with other ideologies. For example, radical right populism (as in the cases of the Dutch Party for Freedom or French Front National/National Rally) combines populism with nativism and authoritarianism (Mudde 2007), while left populism (as in the cases of the Spanish Podemos or Greek Syriza) tends to combine populism with socialism. It is these supporting, 'fuller' ideologies that give body and meaning to the subjects of the people and the elite within populism – as a result, a 'pure' populism without these other ideologies would be borderline meaningless, as the 'emptiness' of the subjects of the people and the elite *need* 'filling' from said complementary ideologies. As Mudde and Rovira Kaltwasser note, 'populism almost always appears attached to other ideological elements, which are crucial for the promotion of political projects that are appealing to a broader public' (2017, p. 6). This understanding of 'thin' and 'thick' ideologies is derived from the work of British political theorist, Michael Freeden (1996, 2003), whose 'morphological' approach to ideology sees ideologies as 'distinctive configurations of political concepts' that 'create specific conceptual patterns from a pool of indeterminate and unlimited combinations' (Freeden 1996, p. 4).

There are several issues with this approach when it comes to attempting to understand the potentiality of populism within political meritocracies like China and Singapore. First, given that the approach sees populism as an ideology, it tends to be put to use to primarily understand populist *parties*, as these are the political actors we tend to most associate with propagating, developing, and spreading ideologies – and more to the point, they often present the most definitive, easily accessible, and practical outlines of ideologies[1] in the form of their party manifestoes, which have a long history of being studied in political science. This view of populism being associated with parties certainly makes a lot of sense in the European context, with many countries, especially those with well-established multi-party systems, having clearly identifiable populist parties. However, it is less useful in making sense of populism in a less clearly-demarcated party landscape, or in identifying populist currents in terms of *intra-party* clashes or on a social movement level, which as we shall see in the next chapter, are arguably the most visible manifestations of populism in China and Singapore today.

Second, scholars working under the ideational approach tend to see populism as a binary category: one clearly 'is' or 'is not' a populist. It does not make sense, for such scholars, to see political actors, parties, or movements as 'somewhat' populist: the name of the game is to be able to *label* political actors as definitively populist (or not), rather than entertain the idea of populism being a degreeist, less-or-more category. While again, this may be useful in terms of identifying 'obvious' cases of populism, it is less useful for identifying borderline cases of the phenomenon, which may utilize populism in a non-uniform or inconsistent manner, or incipient cases of populism, where cases may not yet be 'full-blown' examples of the phenomenon, but very well may be developing in this direction. Again, the examples of what we understand as populism in China and Singapore that we discuss in this book likely fall under the latter category: they surely are not on the level of the likes of no-brainer cases of populism like Donald Trump or Hugo Chávez, but they should also not be dismissed out of hand given how anti-elite hatred and pro-people sentiment is fomenting to a serious degree.

On a wider level, the ideational approach has come under serious criticism from Freeden (2017) himself, who has questioned the stretching of his theoretical framework to understand populism. Freeden has argued that populism should not and cannot be understood as an ideology, not even as a very thin one. He contends that it is:

> simply ideologically too scrawny even to be thin! … A thin-centred ideology implies that there is potentially more than the centre, but the populist core is all there is; it is not a potential centre for something broader or more inclusive. It is emaciatedly thin rather than thin-centred.
>
> (Freeden 2017, p. 3)

Here, he asserts that the categories of a discourse, style, or mode of language may be more useful for understanding populism.

The second central approach in the populism literature is the strategic approach. This view sees populism as a particular strategy, mode of organization, or type of political mobilization used by political leaders. Whereas the ideational approach views populism as something of a feature or characteristic of political actors (that is, it is something that political actors believe, or at least purport to believe or hold as a worldview or set of attitudes), those who follow the strategic approach see it as something that is *done* – as Jansen (2011, p. 75) argues, populism is 'a mode of political practice' in this regard. These authors are thus less interested in leaders' purported beliefs or even in their discourse or language, and more so in the ways that 'how they pursue and sustain power' (Weyland 2017, p. 50). This focus on these instrumental methods can be seen in the central definition utilized under this approach, Weyland's (2001, p. 14) conception of populism as 'as a political strategy through which a personalistic leader seeks or exercises government power based on direct, unmediated, uninstitutionalized support from large numbers of mostly unorganized followers'. Consonant definitions have also been developed by Roberts (2015), Barr (2009), and Jansen (2011).

As can be seen, the role of the leader is paramount in this approach to populism. While the previous mentioned approach tends to ascribe populism primarily to parties (although we also can see it in the ideologies of leaders and movements), the strategic approach explicitly argues that 'populism is a political strategy that revolves around an individual politician. Specifically, populism rests on personalistic leadership' (Weyland 2017, p. 56). More so, authors working under this approach focus on how the personalist leader is able to bypass traditional intermediary institutions likes parties or clientelist networks, instead appealing to their followers in an 'unmediated', semi-direct way that stresses their closeness to the people.

Those who utilize this approach have almost exclusively applied it to cases in the Global South (for example, Kenny 2017; Resnick 2014), with a particular concentration on populism in Latin America (for example, Jansen 2017; Roberts 2003; Weyland 2001, 2003). In this regard, it has been useful for making sense of populism in political systems that are not necessarily established liberal democracies, but rather often hybrid regimes. As such, at first glance it could potentially be useful for analysing populism in political meritocracies like China and Singapore, which clearly fall outside of the liberal democracy category. However, on closer inspection, this approach is not suitable in this regard for two main reasons. First, the approach relies on the assumption that populism only emerges in political environments with relatively weak institutions or underdeveloped party systems – something that Weyland himself acknowledges when noting that this approach does not travel well to the European context, given that 'the longstanding prevalence of fairly well-organized, program-oriented parties in much of Europe leaves limited room for populist movements' (Weyland 2017, p. 62) under his definition. While China and Singapore may not be liberal democracies, they certainly do not have weakly organized parties – the CCP and PAP are highly programmatic, well-organized political machines, rather than just being the kind of personalist vehicles that this approach narrowly associates with populism. Second, its focus on just the personalist leader, which may make sense in terms of interpreting the actions of Xi Jinping or Bo Xilai, puts to the side the potential of populist movements to rise, or the existence of populist discourses in the wider population, which we believe are two of the likely manifestations of populism that may arise in political meritocracies. On a broader level, the approach's core definition could be applied to 'other organizations, such as religious or labour-based parties and millenarian movements, [which] also have charismatic leaders and/or low levels of institutionalization early in their organizational life cycle and may seek to change the political system, yet we do not necessarily consider them populist' (Hawkins 2010, p. 168), leaving us in the situation in which this approach seems simultaneously both too narrow and too loose to be of utility here.

This leaves us with the third approach to populism that is utilized in the academic literature: the discursive-performative approach. This approach views populism as a mode of speaking, acting, or constructing political subjects. A few different terms are used to describe populism that fall under this broad approach. One strand sees populism as a *discourse*, a *discursive frame* or *language* that pits the people against the elite, with a particular focus on how these political identities are characterized, identified, interpellated, and constructed (see, for example, Aslanidis 2016b; Laclau 2005; Panizza 2005; Stavrakakis and Katsambekis 2014; Wodak 2015). Another strand goes a step further, and sees populism not only in discursive terms, but as a mode of *political style* or *performance* that also encompasses particular non-verbal performative, aesthetic, and bodily dimensions. For example, Ostiguy sees populism as the 'flaunting of the low' in politics, and argues that his conception of the anti-populist 'high' and populist 'low':

> have to do with ways of relating to people; as such, they go beyond 'discourses' as words. They certainly include issues of accent, levels of language, body language, gestures, and ways of dressing. And as a way of relating to people, they also encompass the way of making decisions, in politics.
>
> (Ostiguy 2017, p. 77)

Moffitt has made a similar argument, calling populism a distinct *political style* – a term he uses to refer to 'the repertoires of embodied, symbolically mediated performance made to audiences that are used to create and navigate the fields of power that comprise the political' (Moffitt 2016, p. 38) – made up of three central features. The first is an appeal to the people versus the elite, whereby the people are understood as 'both the central audience of populists, as well as the subject that populists attempt to 'render-present' through their performance' (Moffitt 2016, p. 43), while the elite are seen as the group who frustrate, steal, or stand in the way of the people's rightful position of power. The second is 'bad manners', which refers to the way that populists cut against so-called 'appropriate' ways that politicians are 'supposed' to act. This can include the coarsening of political rhetoric, the flaunting of procedures, the use of political incorrectness, or even being more 'colourful' than other politicians in terms of their demonstrativeness or public persona. The third is the performance of crisis, breakdown, or threat, by which Moffitt refers to the way that populists not only get 'their impetus from the perception of crisis, breakdown or threat', but actively aim 'to induce crisis through dramatisation and performance' (Moffitt 2016, p. 45).

Uniting most of the authors working under this approach is the influence of the work of Ernesto Laclau (1977, 2005). Laclau's aim was to develop a theory of populism that would move beyond 'mainly sociologistic categories, which address the group, its constitutive roles and its functional determinations, to the underlying logics that make these categories possible' (Laclau 2000, p. xi). In more common language, what this means is that Laclau did not see groups or identities like the people or the elite as relatively 'pre-existing' with an automatic social base, but instead was focused on how such groups were discursively (and thus politically) formed in the first place. He was interested, then, in how the divides between the people and the elite were set up; who was able to police such boundaries; and how such political identities shifted and changed over time. Those who focus on performance under this approach are thus not only interested in the 'surface' aspects of populism (in terms of aesthetics and style), but also in the power of *performativity* in the sense used by Austin (1975) and Butler (1990): that is, how do words and discourse *do things* to the world? How does the discursive constitution of the people against the elite change political reality?

The discursive-performative approach shares similarities to the strategic approach in that it sees populism as a practice – something that is *done* rather than an inherent property or feature of a political actor. As Bonikowski and Gidron put it, populism should be seen 'as an attribute of the message and not the speaker' (2016a, p. 9). As such, scholars using this approach see populism not as a black-and-white binary category – where certain political leaders, parties, and movements 'are' definitively populist or not – but as a gradational concept, whereby they are interested in the grey zone by which political actors can be more or less populist in terms of frequency or intensity over different periods of time. As a result, this arguably more flexible approach to the phenomenon has made it applicable to a more global set of cases of populism than other approaches: whereas ideational approaches have been limited primarily to the European, Latin American, and North American contexts, and the strategic approach to the Global South, the discursive-performative approach has no such limits, having been applied to places as varied as the Philippines (Curato 2017), South Africa (Mbete 2015), and the US (Bonikowski and Gidron 2016b) – indeed, Moffitt's work sees it applied to 28 leaders from all five continents (Moffitt 2016).

This approach thus has important advantages when it comes to understanding and analysing populism in political meritocracies like China and Singapore. First, its proven 'travelability' means that it makes sense in a variety of contexts, including ones that do not fit the traditional liberal-democratic mould – but importantly in our case, also may not meet the 'developing democracy' characteristics to which the strategic approach to populism tends to be applied – two categories that neither China nor Singapore clearly fit into. Second, while binary approaches to populism are fine for capturing 'clear-cut' cases of populism that no analyst is likely to question, the gradational aspect of the discursive-performative approach is able to capture those cases that may not be so black-and-white. For example, while no-one could seriously call the CCP a 'populist party' in the vein of many European populist radical right parties, one can, as we will show, identify particular leaders and tendencies *within* the party that utilize or embody the populist style as outlined here.[2] The same can be said of the PAP – while they are by no means a populist party, there have been aspects of their political communication in recent years that has been rightly interpreted through a populist lens. Treating populism as both a gradational property *and* seeing it as something that is done and practiced rather than as a particular set property or attribute of a political actor thus allows us to move beyond just identifying certain cases as populist or not, and to instead tease out the populist elements at play in the political communication and discourse of a wide range of political actors – sometimes from unexpected sources – in a more nuanced manner. In light of this, we choose to adopt the definition of populism as a political style developed by Moffitt (2016) laid out above, given that it ties together both the discursive and performative aspects of populism central to this approach in a clear and simple way to guide our analysis in this text.

Having outlined the conceptual framework we intend to utilize in order to understand populism, it is worth closing this chapter by reflecting on why and how populism is construed as a threat in the first place before moving on to our analysis in the next chapter. There is ample academic literature on the potential – and in some cases, very real – threat that populism presents to liberal democracies (see, for example, Mounk 2018; Müller 2016; Rummens 2017; Urbinati 2017), with authors pointing to populism's tendency to reject pluralism, its homogenous view of the people, its capture of independent institutions like courts and the press, its lack of respect for individual rights, its delegitimization of the opposition, and the destabilizing impact of populism's constant courting of crises (Moffitt 2015). However, what about the cases of political meritocracies like China and Singapore, which do not fit into the liberal democracy box? Populism represents a 'threat' to these systems in different ways. First, populism presents a threat to the Chinese government's authoritarian regime by fomenting resentment against the elite in the name of the people. This can have the effect of, first, undermining faith in the political meritocratic system that undergirds China's political culture; second, undermining faith in the CCP elites who are entrusted to run the country; and third, amplifying pro-democracy voices within China that demand that more power be given to the people. As Mudde and Rovira Kaltwasser (2017, p. 88) note in this regard when it comes to authoritarian regimes:

> Because it helps articulate demands of popular sovereignty and majority rule, which call into question existing forms of state repression, populism contributes to the formation of a 'master frame' through which opposition leaders can mobilize (all) those opposed to the regime.

In Singapore, the situation is somewhat different given that the city-state does indeed hold somewhat free elections (albeit ones heavily stacked in favour of the ruling PAP), and citizens have more civil liberties than in China. As such, the potential 'populist threat' goes two ways. First, like in China, populism can present a challenge to the hegemony of the ruling party if anti-elite and pro-people sentiment is allowed to reach a tipping point. This could potentially see demands for more political competition and space for public dissent in Singaporean political life, thus contributing to further democratization within the country. On the other hand, if the PAP leadership itself were to take up the populist style in a serious and consistent manner, the directionality of the populist 'threat' could go the other way, with the (limited) civil liberties of Singaporeans coming under further threat in the name of a repressive leader willing to crack down on minorities in the alleged name of the people.

Yet as we have seen, political meritocracy is presented as a potential bulwark to populism in the first place – either stunting its rise or addressing the concerns that populism draws upon in order to rob it of its 'demand'. So does the populist 'threat' actually concern political meritocracies? Can – and does – the populist political style exist in today's political meritocracies? We turn to these questions in the next chapter, considering the gaps between ideal and reality of political meritocracies, and how populism actually manifests in places like China and Singapore.

Notes

1 Beyond, obviously, the ur-texts of different ideologies like the works of Marx, Mill, Proudhon, and so on.
2 The same argument could be made about the Republican Party under the Trump presidency. While the Republican Party is not (yet, at least) a clear-cut case of a populist radical right party, there is little doubt that Donald Trump himself is a populist leader. This makes perfect sense under a discursive-performative reading of populism, but runs into trouble if adopting a strict ideational approach to the phenomenon.

2 Populism's cure?

Taken together, it is perhaps not entirely apparent given our overview of political meritocracy and populism in the previous chapter how the former has the potential to act as a buffer against the latter – indeed, at first pass, one might even conclude that what political meritocracy does is actually sow the seeds that inflame and invite populism – far from its intended purpose. This is because in a political meritocracy, the crucial divide between the people and the elite that underpins populism clearly and obviously favours the elite, not the people. The elite should not only hold sovereign power in a political meritocracy; the entire system of governance insists that they must *rule over* the people and protect them from their basest political instincts. For most populists, this scenario is exactly what has produced the many political problems faced by Western democracies today – a situation in which popular sovereignty has become increasingly undermined by and ceded to an unelected and powerful elite, who then become the source of all the people's woes (Moffitt 2016; Mudde and Kaltwasser 2017). Make no mistake, the populists would say, it is the elite, not the people, who have wreaked havoc on society. And herein lies the problem: what angers populists is precisely the predicament that political meritocracy seeks to enshrine. In other words, the political meritocratic ideal – that the 'common wisdom' of the people, so often championed by populist leaders, is jettisoned for expert guidance and technocratic governance – is at its core the source of populist revulsion.

But is this actually the case? Is it correct, or enough, to simply conclude that political meritocracy offers no defence against the threat of populism? In this chapter, we demonstrate that the answer to this question is more complex than first appearances might suggest. Yes, political meritocracy's elite-driven system does appear on the surface to fuel populist discontent. Yet, as we will argue in this chapter, this is perhaps too simplistic a reading of how political meritocracy works. In this regard, we claim that political meritocracy is less defined by a single-minded pursuit of elite-driven technocratic governance than the unique blend of virtue, social skills, and intellect – the three key attributes of meritocratic political leadership. It is these attributes that, together and in this order, scholars such as Bell use to base their arguments about political meritocracy's capacity to weather populist uprisings. But far from where the story ends, there is also a flipside to political meritocracy's relationship with populism that we also seek to highlight in this chapter. Indeed, against the backdrop of claims that political meritocracy offers a defence against the threat of populism, we also document the mounting empirical evidence and developments that highlight the creeping presence of populist forces in supposedly meritocratic China and Singapore. In doing this, our objective is to emphasize the very real gap that currently exists between the ideal and reality of political meritocracy, and to address the argument that, as the gap closes, we should expect to see a corresponding decrease of populist politics in political meritocracies.

Political meritocracy's defence against the threat of populism

At the outset, it is necessary to concede an important point: elitist technocracy – or elite-driven technocratic governance – does not so much assuage populist resentment as arouse it. The rule of experts that is the foundation of Singapore's political meritocracy – a model that China's political leaders have long admired and sought to replicate across Mainland China (Ortmann and Thompson 2014; Ho 2018) – is not a bulwark against populist uprising, but a potential source of it. This is a claim that has been clearly demonstrated in the West, where the recent success of populists is often interpreted as a backlash against depoliticized technocracy. As Sandel (2018, p. 354) has argued in no uncertain terms, the 'populist uprising' in the US was an unambiguous 'rebuke for a technocratic approach to politics that is tone deaf to the resentments of people who feel the economy and the culture have left them behind'. The rise of Trump in 2016 was at least in part due to the modern character of the Democratic Party, which has become 'a party of a technocratic liberalism more congenial to the professional classes than to the blue-collar and middle-class voters who once constituted its base' (Sandel 2018, p. 354). Owing to the so-called death of expertise that scholars such as Nichols have written about, and the deeper social malaise which has sought to reject and unseat established knowledge, facts, and rationality, populists in the West have waged an all-too-successful war against technocratic elites on behalf the 'poorly educated' people, to borrow Trump's words (Nichols 2017, p. 213). None of this bodes well for the argument that political meritocracy offers a better defence than democracy against the rise of populism. Indeed, if one of political meritocracy's supposed central cornerstones – elitist technocracy – actually *fuels* populist unrest, then what hope does it really have to *block* populist leaders and politics?

What we want to argue in this section is that, while important, the exclusive focus on elitist *technocracy* perhaps skews or misunderstands what political *meritocracy* is about in its entirety. Yes, populists detest the elite and they distrust technocratic governance. However that, on its own, is only one aspect of political meritocracy. Not only that, we will demonstrate that it is arguably the least important aspect of political meritocracy as well as theorized by Bell.

This is the case because, unlike a purely technocratic system of governance, which only emphasizes intellect, rationality, and expertise, political meritocracy is structured in such a way so that all three attributes of political leadership – intellect, social skills, and virtue – are emphasized. This is something that Bell underscores when seeking to distinguish political meritocracy from other systems of governance. For him, what is most crucial in a political meritocracy is having mechanisms in place to ensure leaders and decision-makers 'be above average on *all three dimensions*' (Bell 2016, p. 108, our emphasis). The rationale here is that leaders and government officials who possess all these attributes – rather than just one or two of these attributes – will not only likely make for good rulers; they will also have a greater awareness of social issues and an aptitude for empathy with those they lead. Oftentimes, political leaders require emotional intelligence and social awareness to understand the difference between what the people want and what they 'require' and, importantly, how to implement the latter without demeaning the former. Given that politics is not science and political reform does not occur in a vacuum, the only way for leaders to effectively serve the people is to be among them. Whereas a purely technocratic system of governance, overseen by detached experts, might be driven only by ends – the people be damned, as long as the 'correct' goals and outcomes are achieved – a meritocratic system theoretically better connects ends with means. Such measures should help reduce the people's sense of powerlessness and alienation from government. In doing so, they should also help reduce, even if they do not altogether eliminate, the divisions between the ruling elite and the common citizen. When this occurs, elites and expertise are put in their place, giving political meritocracy greater political to ward off the challenges of populism.

But this is only the first part of the answer to why political meritocracy might offer better guarantees against the rise of meritocracy than elitist technocracy. A more important reason lies not so much in the equal amalgam of political meritocracy's three attributes of political leadership than the hierarchy between them. According to Bell, not all meritocratic attributes should be regarded as equal when judging good leadership and governance. There is an important meritocratic hierarchy at work. While a strictly technocratic system elevates the importance of intellectual ability over all else, atop the meritocratic system sits the attribute of virtue. Indeed, political meritocracies are distinct in that, without a desire for and proven track record in moral quality, righteousness, uprightness, and con-scientiousness, no amount of intellectual or social savviness is likely to be enough to qualify a politician for top-level leadership. Put differently, it is virtue that enables political leaders to use their intellect and social skills to the greatest effect. Lacking a 'desire to serve the public', Bell (2016, p. 108) writes, 'a political leader can put his or her intelligence and social skills to disastrous uses', as history can attest. Indeed, while it is fair to say that no political system will ever be entirely free from populist urges, Bell (2017b) believes that virtuous political leaders will be able to better respond to the people's needs – not blindly but with a view of all those affected. That virtuous politics should essentially be a people-centric pol-itics thus should help to assuage populist discontent. Moreover, because virtuous politics puts a premium on character, it means that political leaders who are driven exclusively by self-interests or the interests of a minority – whether that minority be a particularly exclusionary rendering of 'the people' or 'the elite' – will likely experience limited political success.

Once virtue is established, the next attribute in the meritocratic hier-archy is social skills. A political leader who is unable or unwilling to relate to and understand the people – and their fellow leaders – is likely to be an ineffective leader culpable of alienating and angering large sectors of society. Even the best policies crafted by the sharpest political minds have missed the mark, or done more harm than good, when their benefactors could not understand or relate to what was done on their behalf. A socially-aware leader acts less as the people's conduit in this context and more as a bridge between the epicentres of power and the political periphery. However, this attribute, as some have argued, could actually become a cor-rupting force for politicians and be susceptible for exploitation by popu-lists under the right circumstances. As Kevin Wong (2018, p. 893) points out, the advantage of selecting and evaluating political leaders based on performance is to 'unfetter politics from the caprice of voters'. Yet by ele-vating social skills, and thereby the importance of leaders' personal appeal and charisma, a meritocratic system not only undermines performance legitimacy, it also opens the way for the type of popularity contests among political leaders that is at the heart of populist politics (and some might cynically argue, modern democratic politics in general). For Wong (2018, p. 894), the inherent danger in emphasizing social skills is that it would foster in leaders a 'sympathy (or susceptibility) to the emotions of those around them', which in turn could 'cloud a leader's ability to render impartial decisions, preventing them from focusing exclusively on the relative strength of the evidence'. While Wong's logic is hard to dispute from a strictly technocratic viewpoint, for our purposes at least, completely ignoring the desires of the governed also undermines virtuous politics, which can then fuel the type of populist anger against technocratic governance that we have already alluded to.

This then leaves the final and lowliest attribute in Bell's meritocratic hierarchy: intellectual ability. Though the positioning of leaders' intellectual ability at the bottom of the meritocratic hierarchy may come as a surprise to those more familiar with technocracy or even economic meritocracy, it should be clear by now that political meritocracy is distinct in important ways. As noted earlier, for example, while meritocracy is often understood simply as IQ plus effort, a political meritocracy is in fact a system that seeks to put intellect and expertise in their rightful place. In such a system, which selects leaders based on merits and performance, it is necessary to have in place safeguards that stop those leaders from abusing their power or harming the people's needs. For Bell (2017b), this is not only why virtue and social awareness have to trump intellectual ability in a political meritocracy. It is also why fighting corruption and establishing Confucian moral education have been atop of the Chinese Communist Party's political priorities of the last decade. By providing checks and balances such as these – though others are obviously needed too – the system thus seeks to channel and tame intellect in non-hubristic ways. In this regard, leaders need not be Nobel Laureates or Fields Medallists; they only need to possess sufficient IQ and technical expertise to appropriately implement policies deemed necessary by their EQ. To distil this simply: no matter how intellectually brilliant or capable a leader may be, they are of limited use in a political meritocracy if they are not also humble and approachable. Part of the reason why populists have agitated for political change in the West is because of the perceived arrogance and detachment of technocratic elites who, it is claimed, do little to stand with, or in the shoes of those they govern. Though they may have superior intelligence and technical expertise, they are ineffectual because they are neither trusted nor understood by the people. It is this reason why virtue has to sit atop the meritocratic hierarchy and intellect at the bottom – because long-term trust can only be earned through moral strength, not through superior intellect. That is what ultimately separates technocrats from *junzi*. Whereas the former is driven by intellect alone, the latter seeks virtue to guide intellect.

We believe that understanding this hierarchy not only offers important insights into the ideal of political meritocracy; it also reveals how the system of political meritocracy may help prevent the rise of populist forces in society. Specifically, in what follows, we draw on this hierarchy to highlight what we argue are the three key reasons supporting the claim that political meritocracy can theoretically ward off populist success.

The first reason is perhaps the most important and also the most obvious: unlike electoral democracies, only a very particular type of political figure will likely achieve political success and be selected for top leadership roles in a political meritocracy. Indeed, if the three meritocratic attributes are used as the basis for selecting and promoting political leaders, the likelihood that populists such as a Donald Trump will ever rise to the pinnacle of political power should be drastically reduced, if not altogether eliminated. Though much has been written about the American president's 'campaign against established knowledge' and his inability 'to answer even rudimentary questions about policy' (Nichols 2017, p. 211), the more damning indictment from the perspective of political meritocracy is that Trump and the popular electoral system that brought him to power not only tolerated but *rewarded* the openly debased behaviour that helped the former reality TV mogul amass his fame and fortune. Indeed, Trump's 'bashing and pummeling' (Brooks 2016) style of politics, so favoured by populists, is precisely what would disbar him from consideration for top political posts in a political meritocracy, without even mentioning his absolute lack of political expertise and experience. Though socially savvy, at least among those Americans disenchanted by mainstream politics, Trump's utter lack of credentials when it comes to virtue and intellect would most probably see him languish at the lower political echelons in a political meritocracy.

But, of course, Trump is not the only populist who would fall short on this front. Research on the stylistic and discursive appeal of populists has shown that their 'non-virtuous' behaviour is at the core of their popular appeal: the 'low' (Ostiguy 2017) or 'bad manners' (Moffitt 2016) of the likes of figures like Rodrigo Duterte, Nigel Farage, or Hugo Chávez are presented as flying in the face of the po-faced 'virtuous' behaviour of mainstream politicians. Even those populist figures whose manners may be more moderate or 'professional' – such as the likes of Marine Le Pen or Geert Wilders – still rely on the shock tactic of overt political incorrectness, breaking taboos, and 'saying the unsayable' in order to gain attention and clearly delineate themselves from 'mainstream' politicians. And while there is undoubtedly virtue in being the people's champion and holding elites to account, it is important to stress that this frequently occurs at the expense of some of society's most vulnerable members, with populists often targeting those who are not part of 'the people' for scapegoating, punishment, ridicule, or abuse – again, a not particularly virtuous mode of leadership or political representation. The point here is that, while many populist leaders may be able to satisfy one or two (or even, in rare cases, all three) of the meritocratic attributes, very few will be able to do so according to the meritocratic hierarchy that emphasizes virtue first, social skills second, and intellectual ability last. For this reason, as those like Bell have suggested, it is very implausible that a system structured on the ideals of political meritocracy will elevate populist political officials and leaders.

The second reason why a political meritocracy may help ease mass populist discontent has to do with the ideal of meritocracy more broadly. At its core, meritocracy is a system of social mobility that rewards individuals not on the basis of birth or class, but by them possessing or demonstrating a set of valued merits. More than this, there is an innate principle of meritocracy which holds that through effort or hard work, individuals can achieve more than those who may be naturally talented yet do little to cultivate these attributes. No matter how lowly or disadvantaged an individual may be by birth or circumstance, then, the ideal of meritocracy offers them a path for upward mobility and success.

But how does this help prevent populist discontent? Simply put, the prospect of upward political mobility in a political meritocracy – of entering the elite based on individual merit rather than pedigree or financial background – can undermine the populist claim against entrenched elitism and inequality in society. As research shows, populist resentment is often sparked by perceptions of economic and social inequality and the widening chasms separating the so-called winners of globalization from the losers (Mellen 2017; Norris and Inglehart 2019). To this end, populist leaders and parties have been most successful when tapping into the people's fears of downward social mobility and connecting this to contempt for corrupt elites – and in many regards, populist complaints against elite corruption and collusion have been entirely justified. In the Latin American context, for example, populism has been an understandable reaction to hollowed-out, corrupt, and elite-driven political systems that have otherwise purported to be democratic, while in Europe, populists have been very effective at revealing the 'democratic deficit' at the heart of elite projects like the European Union and the economic governance of the Troika (Ivarsflaten 2008; Taggart 2004). In such environments, the populist demand for increased accountability and transparency is entirely reasonable. Simultaneously, populist actors have offered hope to the people of having their excluded voice heard in the corridors of power – something that has been most clear in the experiences of 'inclusive populism' in the Global South, where figures like Evo Morales and Thaksin Shinawatra have given voice to previously excluded sectors in their respective societies (Mudde and Kaltwasser 2012); or in the Global North in the 'Movements of the Squares' of the 2010s, whereby Occupy Wall Street in the US, the Indignados movements of Spain and Greece sought to give voice to 'the people' who had been economically locked out of power (Aslanidis 2016a; Gerbaudo 2017).

While merit can still be regarded as an unwarranted privilege by those lacking it (Mavrogordatos 1997, p. 19), the idea that society's political elite are drawn from the people in fair and just ways has the potential to mitigate populist resentment against social inequality and entrenched elitism. Though elitism obviously remains, having an elite drawn from the people in a 'fair' (or at least transparent) way helps bestow a sense of justice and legitimacy from the perspective of society's underprivileged and left behind. Indeed, the notion of meritocracy broadly conceived is one that functions to allow 'low status group members to dream about improving their social status, economic class, and place in the hierarchy, implanting the ideology that everyone has a chance of succeeding if they cultivate the required abilities', rather than just, for example, being wealthy or having the right connections (Kim and Choi 2017, p. 112). But empowering society's lowest members not only offers hope to others of a better future. It ideally ensures the political elite are comprised, at least in part, of people who can understand the plight of the people. As such, where it has been practiced effectively, meritocracy has been a powerful engine of 'upward mobility for maintaining social order and calming social unrest' (Kim and Choi 2017, p. 112). By offering 'equality of opportunity' to all, it theoretically bridges the cultural, economic, and political chasms dividing the people from the elite.

Whereas our second reason focused primarily on meritocracy, our third and final reason touches on one of the key tenets of populism. As researchers of populism have long noted, populists have been at their most convincing when exploiting a sense of societal crises as justification for acting brashly and breaking with the status quo (Laclau 1977; Roberts 1995; Stavrakakis *et al.* 2018). So much is this the case that some scholars have posited the performance or promotion of crisis as a core feature of populism (Moffitt 2015; Rooduijn 2014). For populists, crises can be related to any number of phenomena, including (but not limited to) the breakdown between citizens and their representatives, immigration, economic difficulties, perceived injustice, social transformation, or other political, cultural, and economic maladies. By invoking crisis, populists aim to radically simplify the terms and terrain of political debate to allow for often abrupt and short-term policy responses versus the 'slow politics' (Saward 2015) of negotiation and deliberation (we can think of Trump's travel ban on a number of Muslim-majority countries in the name of fighting terrorism or Duterte's extra-judicial killing of drug users in the name of a 'war on drugs' here). But when politics becomes so highly instrumentalized and prone to kneejerk decisions, a polity does not so much ward off as court future crises, which provides an ongoing sense of emergency that populism can feed off.

While crisis will always be part of politics and life more broadly, it is clear that rule by those with above average virtue, social skills, and intellectual ability should at least offer society a better chance of steering clear of avoidable crises than if ruled by the inexperienced, ill-tempered, or foolish. This is where political meritocracy's technocratic underpinnings do become particularly helpful. By 'stressing the prominence of expertise in the identification and implementation of objective solutions to societal problems', the political system is ideally suited to identifying and averting crises (Caramani 2017, p. 55). Moffitt (2016, pp. 46–47) outlines the three core differences between populism and technocracy in this regard. First, while populists direct their appeal to the people against the elite, and in doing so, contend that we should place our faith in common sense or the wisdom of the people, technocrats trust specialist training and expertise. Second, while populists tend to utilize 'bad manners' in regards to how they present themselves, speak, or act, aiming to make clear their distance from 'mainstream' politics, technocrats have 'good manners', acting in a so-called 'proper' manner, and drawing on a dry and 'objective' discourse and mode of self-presentation. This divide is also marked by the role of emotions and affect: while populists rely on passionate performances, technocrats aim for emotional neutrality and rationality, with a certain 'remove' from the world of passions. Finally, while populists aim to invoke and perform crisis, technocrats have stability or measured progress as their goal (De la Torre 2013, p. 37). For technocrats, the proper functioning of society is presented as being able to be delivered by those with the requisite knowledge, training, and standing. Factors such as these are frequently cited as reasons why Singapore remains largely devoid of short-sighted and emotional populist politics (Hendrie 2015).

But as we have argued, technocracy alone does not amount to political meritocracy, given that it eschews virtue and social skills. As research demonstrates, technocracy can in fact trigger greater de-politicization and an upswing of anti-political sentiment, which can breed the culture of 'corrosive cynicism' that populism grows from (Flinders 2012, p. 2). Without understanding and caring about people on whose behalf policies are enacted, technocrats can exacerbate the crises that have fuelled populist anger in recent decades. This is why in a political meritocracy, virtue and social awareness govern the intellect, thus positioning the system as ideally able to prevent the crises which can be avoided while dampening the effects of those which cannot.

Political meritocracy and the rise of populism

That is the theory. But what about the reality? Do the two stack up, or diverge, when it comes to political meritocracy? The good news from this perspective is that in political systems broadly structured around the ideal of political meritocracy, populists have had nowhere near the impact they have recently enjoyed in Western democracies, where once fringe movements, parties, and political leaders have come to occupy more central posts in the political landscape. This has decidedly not been the case in China and Singapore – the two best, if far from imperfect, examples of political meritocracies today – where populism continues to remain largely a force mired down on the political periphery. In those contexts, political leaders often like to make a point of contrasting the populist 'scourge' rampaging through the West with the relative stability in their own polities (Reich 2016). Where there are discussions about populism in the East, they are usually about how the rise of populists in the West could affect Asian interests (Haenle and Carothers 2018).

Despite this, to conclude that populist forces are no cause for concern in supposedly meritocratic China and Singapore would also be an over-simplification and empirically inaccurate. There is now evidence to suggest that populism is cropping up, both from the margins and main-stream of political life, in contemporary political meritocracies. Today, as the China expert Elizabeth Perry (2015, p. 905) claims, the increasingly authoritarian Chinese state's frequent mentions of democracy (*minzhu* 民主) are very much underpinned by a populist dream that seeks to (at least theoretically) return power to 'the primacy of the people'. With its origins in the *Book of History*, or *Shujing* (书经), Perry (2015, p. 905) notes that the Communist Party's outwardly paradoxical use of the term is in fact put to work to elevate 'the people' who are seen as 'the sole foundation of the state'. What is more, this is not just the view of a minority of citizens or politicians. Citing a 2011 Chinese Academy of Social Sciences survey on political attitudes, Perry demonstrates that the majority of Chinese citizens see democracy primarily as a mechanism for reflecting the will of the people rather than as an electoral procedure for selecting political leaders. Specifically, as she notes, some 85 per cent of Chinese respondents preferred what she argued was a populist rather than electoral definition of democracy, which emphasized that national leaders 'reflect people's interests, serve the people, and submit to supervision by the people' (Perry 2015, p. 908). Even the best educated respondents, those

who possessed Masters and Doctorates for example, preferred this populist to electoral definition of democracy. If nothing else, Perry's analysis
would contradict the claims that there is widespread support in China for
the ideal of political meritocracy, which posits a very different conception
of leadership (Bell 2017c, p. 98).

Contemporary China now also faces populism in another guise. In
recent years, there has been growing popular support for a 'Chinese populist nationalism' that lauds 'the glorious memory of Imperial China and its
historical legacy' and 'the people's quest for a just social order in the
national context' (Yu 2014, p. 1174; Xu 2001, p. 125). While the rise of
nationalism is not unique to China, Chinese populist nationalism has point-
edly risen in opposition to state nationalism and draws its members from
all economic classes. Guided by a skewed nostalgia for Imperial Chinese
glory, this populist movement has exerted pressure on the Communist
Party to take a more aggressive stance in regional disputes, believing that
'surrounding countries, including Japan, South Korea, and the South-
eastern countries, are ungrateful for the protection provided them by
ancient China and that they have denied and exploited China's historic
legacy' (Yu 2014, p. 1187). Domestically, they have been pushing for a
social order that is more 'people-oriented' and 'Chinese in character' (Xu
2001, p. 125).

Then there is the broader ideological revival that has been spreading
across China. According to Taisu Zhang, Chinese society is beginning to
show signs of a renewed appetite for ideological struggle not seen since
the Tiananmen Square massacre (Zhang 2016). Several of these struggles
have populist overtones to them. To name only one, the New Left represents a loose grouping of neo-Maoists who share a distaste for China's
embrace of neo-liberalism and a deep distrust of the country's intellectual,
technocratic, and elite class who, they claim, are guilty of 'corruption,
egotism, technocratic arrogance, moral decay, and, most viciously, of ...
betraying their country's national interests' (Chandran 2017; Holbig and
Gilley 2010, p. 405). To this extent, the New Left has often been most
effective when calling out economic injustice and condemning China's
economic growth at any cost (He 2015; Anshu *et al.* 2018). Hugely
popular among peasants, workers, and even students, the New Left's
policy agenda seeks to revive the *San Nong*: *nongmin* (peasants), *nongye*
(agriculture), and *nongcun* (rural communities) (Pocha 2005, p. 27).
According to Li He (2009, p. 35), 'liberals view the New Left as nationalist and populist as the latter appeal to masses of the working class by advo-
cating welfare policies and greater governmental control of the economy'.
Emboldened by such movements, China's peasant and rural citizens have
frequently made news in recent years for publicly protesting their plight

and mistreatment at the hand of the ruling elite. Dissent, as Khalid Nadiri (2007, p. 125) writes, has been 'populist in both nature and rhetoric, with protest frequently directed toward corrupt and heavy-handed local CPC officials or the Chinese middle and upper classes'.

However, none of this rivals the populism now emanating from the very top of the CPC leadership. Since coming to power in 2012, Xi has quickly transformed China's political landscape. Though an establishment figure that rose through the ranks of the CPC, Devin Stewart and Jeffrey Wasserstrom (2016) believe that Xi has borrowed heavily from 'domestic and international populist playbooks' to rally the country behind his vision. Even from the start, Xi made appeals to the 'Chinese people' as a 'great people', unlike his predecessor's more 'scientific' approach to governance (Fewsmith 2013). Moreover, one of Xi's cornerstone ideas – the China Dream – has been said to have more than a passing resemblance to Trump's America First policy (Babones 2017). But it goes beyond that. As Joseph Fewsmith (2013, p. 6) argues, 'visions of the China Dream, leading the charge against corruption, and appealing to "socialism with Chinese characteristics" all suggest efforts to shake up the part and bolster legitimacy through populism'. Known affectionately by the Chinese as Papa Xi, popular songs and poems have immortalized the Chinese leader 'as a virtuous husband, a friend to the toiling peasant and an enemy of the corrupt', write Andrew Jacobs and Chris Buckley (2015). Not since Mao's rule, they note, has China seen such an overtly populist leader who radiates charisma and is hailed both as 'Superman and Everyman' (Jacobs and Buckley 2015; Hernandez 2018) – a leader that embodies the difficult balance of displaying both ordinary and extraordinary qualities oft-cited as core to populist leadership (Moffitt 2016, pp. 55–57). Personalistic rule is back with a vengeance in China (Shirk 2018). Of course, all of this is part of the broader 'ideological war' that have seen some Chinese leaders, Xi among them, herald 'Mao not only as the party's founding father, but also as a symbol of its commitment to nationalism and populism', as Taisu Zhang (2016) puts it. Others, such as Yu Jie (2019), claim that what is underpinning Xi's populist tactics is an awareness that the vast economic inequalities and severe environmental devastation created by Deng Xiaoping's reforms have split Chinese society in two, and that this division could soon threaten the 'very survival of the Party leadership'. So while working to shore up his own position and power within the CPC, Xi has had to resort to populist schemes to get the people on side and make the prospect of a ruler for life under a one-party system more palatable. Now empowered to rule for life, Xi thus looks to 'remain a popular force in Chinese politics' as 'China's first populist president' (Babones 2017).

Though significantly smaller both in size and populist influences, Singapore's more developed political meritocracy has not been entirely devoid of populist incursions. Indeed, as it was widely observed at the time, the watershed election of 2011, which shocked many in the People's Action Party and beyond, demonstrated that even so-called anti-populist Singapore was not immune to the allure of populism (or at very least anti-elite sentiment). Though the ruling PAP was returned to power, they registered a historically low 60.14 per cent of the popular vote as opposition parties such as the centre-left Workers' Party gained ground (Matijasevich 2018). This electoral outcome was important not in the sense that it opened the door wide for opposition (and potentially, populist) parties to take hold of power. Rather, and perhaps more interestingly, it pushed the PAP to embrace what for many were a raft of reforms that in the Singaporean context, can be interpreted as 'populist' in substance. Policies initiatives from universal healthcare, senior and low-income citizens' assistance packages, public housing spending, tightening of foreign labour markets and immigration, and more government consultation were proposed as the backbone of a slower, kinder, and gentler Singaporean society. But it was not lost on commentators that what these reforms effectively did was to eschew the PAP's conventional approach, which is to take the long view when implementing policies, and instead saw the PAP opt for short-term 'populist' solutions. For a political party that has defined a system which is today the epitome of political meritocracy in practice, this was a surprising move, and one that fundamentally undermines claims that political meritocracy is structured to weather populist politics. But for Elvin Ong (2013), there is nothing all that surprising about what happened. As he writes:

> From this view, then, my point is that the PAP, as like all other political parties, have always been populist parties at the onset because they seek to maximize their votes. They are as populist now as they are in the past. Ironically, no matter how much PAP politicians may demonize populism or say they disregard public opinion in the past, they do so in order to pander to populism.
>
> (Ong 2013)

Though there are many more examples we could highlight and analyse here, it suffices to say that political meritocracy and populism may not be as anathema to one another as some would have them appear. In China in particular, populism is not simply a political relic of Mao Zedong's political order (Townsend 1977). It remains alive and well in at least a partial form under the rule of Xi. Even in supposedly anti-populist Singapore, the PAP has more than shown its willingness to tap into a diffuse sense of populism when it is politically expedient to do so. As such, we are left with an important question to ponder: how do we reconcile the reality in these 'actually existing' political meritocracies with the proposition that political meritocracy provides safeguards against the onslaught of populist politics?

The advocates of political meritocracy would likely offer two relatively straightforward answers to this question. The first relates to political reality (as opposed to normative theory) itself. Speaking primarily about the current situation in China, for instance, Bell (2016, p. 2; 2013, p. 7) has conceded that China's model of political meritocracy is 'plagued with imperfections' and that the 'process of "meritocratization" in China is an ongoing and unfinished process'. He has been candid, when pushed, about the chasm that currently exists between the ideal of political meritocracy he advocates and the reality of its current application, which is afflicted by problems of factionalism, patronage, corruption, and lack of transparency that serve to separate those within the CPC's inner circle from those unlucky enough to find themselves on the outside. In more recent times, the system now also faces the new question of whether a political merito-cracy can truly be meritocratic if it empowers those with ultimate power to rule for life? These are tricky issues that undermine the meritocratic claims of China's political system. And for the most, those like Bell have conceded this.

This, in part, is why critics of Bell and of political meritocracy have often labelled his account of meritocratic China as 'bogus', a work of fiction, and completely unreflective of current political reality (He 2016; Nathan 2015; Garton Ash 2015). Timothy Garton Ash (2015), in par-ticular, calls into question Bell's exchange with Li Yuanchao about balan-cing intellectual acuity with virtue and social skills mentioned in the previous chapter. Although admitting that 'neither Daniel nor I were actu-ally behind those closed doors ... we know a lot about how the CCP works – and it doesn't work like that'. The general thrust of critiques like Garton Ash's is that China is not a true political meritocracy, which is why it experiences the upheavals and problems – populist and otherwise – that it does. This observation is consistently reflected in scholarship that exposes the contradiction between the 'hierarchical conformity commanded by the political institutions' and the 'private search of bureaucrats for individual-istic interests through particularistic ties of *guanxi*' in Chinese politics (Zhang 2015, p. 274). Other studies have been more damning, revealing that the balance clearly tips in favour of *guanxi* over merit in determining upward political mobility (Hui and Gore 2017, p. 16; Zeng 2013; Li 2011). Li Hui and Lance Gore (2017, p. 16) put it unequivocally in their study when they concluded the 'single most important factor in career advancement – "recognition and appreciation" from superiors – is associated more with patronage than merit'. As for those without the right connections, corruption has often presented itself as a solution to those who fail to achieve success in the country's demanding civil service examinations, which on average admits only about 1 per cent of all applicants (Zhang 2015, p. 279). Singapore's more established political meritocracy has also created problems that undermine its meritocratic credentials. Whereas the ideal of political meritocracy is supposed to operate as a political mobility mechanism, Singapore's political system has more often than not created a self-perpetuating political elite that freezes the political status quo (*The Economist* 2015). Given this, Benjamin Wong and Xunming Huang (2010, p. 538) claim that, the growing popular 'perception that the elites have benefited disproportionately from the system or that not all their privileges are justified is therefore not without merit'.

Conceding several of these points, Bell's (2015) position has been that political meritocracy, especially in China, remains an ideal that is still very theoretical in parts (Fish 2015). Even so, Bell (2016, p. xvii) maintains that for China's political system at least, progress has come in leaps and bounds since Mao's disastrous populist experiment, and that this is an achievement not to be downplayed even as it faces new challenges such as the changes which now allow Xi to stay in power for life. For all its problems, then, he says that '[m]eritocracy is where mainstream political culture is in China' today (*China Daily* 2018). Moreover, as Bell (2017a, p. 315) has written, the 'large gap between the ideal and the current situation' can also be politically valuable as 'the ideal – which today is effectively based on meritocracy rather than the old Marxist dogma – can still help us understand and evaluate the Chinese political reality'. To this end, the continued presence of populist undercurrents in Chinese politics can be interpreted as part and parcel of China's working towards this ideal – and as this ideal becomes closer to reality, the prospects of populism should lessen. This is a point that has been implicitly made by other scholars since Bell's defence. For those like Ho (2018) and Matijasevich (2018), it is clear that Singapore has a vastly more developed political meritocracy than China. Indeed, 'China's emulation of Singapore's patterns and approach to governance remains partial at best' (Ho 2018, p. 89).

The second answer that champions of political meritocracy would likely offer to the question of how we reconcile the problematic political reality with the proposition that political meritocracy provides safeguards against the onslaught of populist politics touches on the complexities and imperfections of politics itself. In a 2017 Chinese interview, for instance, Bell (2017b) responded to a question about Trump's shock 2016 election victory and how 'good politics' might help stop populism by saying:

'Good politics cannot be completely free from populism.' This underscores an important point that applies not only to political meritocracy: no political system is ever perfect; all are susceptible to challenge, distortion, corruption, or downfall. There is always a gap between reality and ideal. As established democracies have demonstrated recently, even mature political systems with time tested checks and balances can sometimes be no guarantee against the threat of corrosive forces (Levitsky and Ziblatt 2018; Chou 2013; Keane 2009). Bell's (2016, p. x) *The China Model* is, in part, an attempt to remind Western readers of this point and to 'desacralize' the ideal that one person, one vote is the only or even the best procedure of selecting political leaders and ensuring good governance.

Even so, Bell seems to suggest that political meritocracy's emphasis on virtuous politics, even if imperfect in practice, potentially sets it apart from other political systems when it comes to stopping or avoiding populism. Speaking indirectly in defence of China's meritocratic model, he invokes the all-affected principle by noting:

> The best way for a virtuous political system to avoid populism is that the political hierarchy responds well to the needs of the people (not blindly responding to the needs of the people: rulers in virtuous politics need to consider the interests of all those affected by the policy, such as future generations and people abroad).
>
> (Bell 2017b)

Moreover, to avoid becoming self-serving elites, who then become targets of populist backlash, leaders chosen because of their 'superior ability and good virtues rather than family and class backgrounds' must continue to 'serve the interests of the ruled' (Bell 2017b). But none of this, he would note, should be taken as absolute guarantee against threats of populism or other political threats – this is just the nature of politics.

Singapore's example is instructive on this point. Despite being in many ways the country's official governing ideology, Tan has noted that political meritocracy continues to be 'negotiated (even struggled over) as different classes and social forces attempt, amid changing circumstances, to forge an unavoidably contradictory consensus on how it might be meaningful for and beneficial to their own lives' (Tan 2008, p. 8). For the most part, Singaporeans operate under a social contract where they forego certain rights and freedoms to politicians and high-ranking civil servants – often characterized as 'talented, selfless, dedicated, and above all extremely competent' – in return for the high standard of living they have become accustomed to (Barr 2016, p. 2; Wong and Huang 2010, p. 528). However, Singapore's brand of virtuous politics has bred its own brand of inequality and resentment, as we have already alluded to. In fact, many believe that political meritocracy has entrenched the PAP as a permanent elite ruling class. Emphasizing merit over pedigree may sound egalitarian, but the reality is that the clear majority of 'Singaporeans are excluded by definition [from elite circles] from the very beginning' (Ortmann and Thompson 2016, p. 43). For Ho Kwon Ping (2015, p. 6), one of the country's leading businessmen, Singapore is at risk of becoming a 'static meritocracy' that creates a 'self-perpetuating elite class'. For Tan (2013, p. 327), there is today a pervasive:

> belief [that] meritocracy has weakened, leaving a strong sense that in its place is now elitism of the kind that focuses on winning and maximizing rewards for the winners and downplaying factors and reasons that limit opportunities for the disadvantaged.

All these factors now mean Singapore is far from immune to the threat of populism. Current inequalities and future crises will spur more citizens, many already alienated from and resentful of the ruling elite, to resist and seek alternatives to the ruling orthodoxy (Huxley 2016; Prakash 2014; Tan 2008). At least some of these alternatives might turn out to be populist.

These caveats are important and go to show that no political system can ever be entirely made foolproof against threats and crises. This is as true of political meritocracy as it is of democracy. But when it comes to the threat of populism, we have demonstrated in this chapter that the advocates of political meritocracy believe it offers unique checks to prevent the widespread rise of populist forces in society. That there are still populist uprisings and echoes in these polities, they argue, has more to do with the current implementation and practice of political meritocracy, not to mention the imperfect nature of politics itself, than with the ideal of political meritocracy. But this is truly the case? Yes, we might be able to accept that no political system can ever be perfect. Yet can we expect that as political meritocracy becomes more 'perfected' in reality it will likewise provide greater barriers against the rise of populism? This is the question we turn to in the next chapter.

3   The populist teleology of meritocracy

It should be clear by now that advocates of political meritocracy like Daniel Bell do not necessarily see the current populist tensions and disturbances in countries such as China and Singapore as a sign of political meritocracy's failings. If anything, Bell's position could be summarized as thus: though politics always has the potential to surprise, exposing even the very 'best' political systems as deficient and problematic in some regards in the process, an established system of political meritocracy should at least *lessen* the prospects of populist challenges. For defenders of political meritocracies, it is thus up to governments and bureaucracies in countries such as China and Singapore, to do better and ensure that reforms continue to advance – rather than undermine – meritocratic ideals in politics.

In this chapter, we put forward a third possible response to the book's central puzzle – why are political meritocracies simultaneously immune and susceptible to populism? – but one that inverts the answer proposed by scholars like Bell. While we agree that no political system that purports to speak for 'the people' can ever be completely free from populism, we draw on the work of Michael Young to make the case that the more established and universal the system of political meritocracy becomes, the more it actually opens the door to populism. To this end, populism can be understood as political meritocracy's 'permanent shadow', to co-opt Jan-Werner Müller's (2016, p. 5) words – a phenomenon that always has the potential to arise in established meritocratic systems, despite what defenders of political meritocracy might claim.

Specifically, we draw on Young's 1958 dystopian story, *The Rise of Meritocracy*, which was not only responsible for coining the term 'meritocracy', but which also portrayed the disenfranchisement, social stratification, and disconnect that would follow as meritocratic ideals became increasingly entrenched into the political, economic, and cultural order, thus leading to populist resentment, and ultimately, revolt. What Young's tale offers us therefore is a critical lesson about the relationship between meritocracy and populism that the advocates of political meritocracy often miss or underplay – that is, one can attempt to make a system more 'just' in terms of processes and how resources and power are distributed, but populists are arguably less motivated by eradicating injustice than inequality – whether perceived or real; economic, political, or cultural. It is for this reason that, in Young's story, only an egalitarian and classless society, where the equal and unequal alike are treated the same, could satisfy the masses in the end. This is also the same reason why, as we argue in this chapter, a political meritocracy will never be free of populist impulses – because it will always contain the seeds of populist discontent.

Populism and the rise – and fall – of meritocracy

It was Michael Young, the twentieth-century British sociologist, Labour politician, and author of the satirical 1958 novel *The Rise of Meritocracy*, who first popularized the term meritocracy in the West. Since that time, whenever there has been talk of meritocracy, Young and *The Rise of Meritocracy* have often found their way into the discussion. Even in *The China Model*, Bell (2016, p. 127) himself acknowledges Young and noted his prediction that 'meritocratically selected leaders would become arrogant and detached from the rest of society'. But what few of these authors have done, Bell included, is to tease out the intrinsic, and crucial, connection that Young draws between meritocracy and populism. Indeed, why Young's *The Rise of Meritocracy* is so central to our own argument here is that it unambiguously predicts, or predicates, that a fully realized meritocracy would eventually sow the seeds of populism.

In Young's story – set in a future United Kingdom, in the year 2033 – achievement has replaced ascription as society's governing ideology. As the only game in town, meritocracy, which stratifies society using the formula 'IQ + effort = merit', meant that power and privilege were now claims that had to be earned rather than inherited. From an early age, all people were thus tested and segregated based on their intelligence. Funnelled into different educational and vocational pathways deemed appropriate to their intellect, the people of this society thus lived out very separate lives not of their own choosing. While the system allowed for some fluidity during its early years, enabling the ambitious and competitive 'to swim from one stream to another', excessive ambition, competition, and flexibility eventually became seen as dangerous to both the system of distributive justice and the new social order as they were gradually perfected (Young 1958, p. 59). But no amount of tightening and perfecting the system was enough to stamp out the bitterness and discontent that grew among those who found themselves at the bottom of the merito-cratic hierarchy. In fact, the more perfected, established and thus segreg-ated the system became, the more dejected the inferiors felt. As Young's (1958, p. 85) narrator tells us, in the past, '[e]ducational injustice enabled people to preserve their illusions, inequality of opportunity fostered the myth of human equality'. That is to say, in a world ruled more by the dic-tates of pedigree, individuals who failed to achieve success could at least blame their predicament on the unjust system or their rotten luck: those who got ahead were simply blessed by the lottery of birth, being born into wealthy or well-connected families or, if not, were fortunate enough to rise above their posts through good schooling and training.

These scapegoats were no longer available to the inhabitants of Young's meritocratic dystopia. With social rank directly, objectively, and scientifi-cally pegged to one's merits, individuals only had themselves to blame for their failures. In this 'justly unequal' society – which had replaced its 'unjustly unequal' predecessor – one's lot was exactly what one rightly deserved (Allen 2011, p. 370). To put it another way, a perfected merito-cracy did not eradicate inequality – only injustice. In fact, the political, economic, and cultural order created and sustained through a meritocracy became predicated solely on an inequality (or hierarchy) that was 'justly' determined – according to merits. This was the 'enduring genius' of mer-itocracy, as Young saw it: the ability to make the 'resulting inequality appear like justice' (Prabhala 2013). As such, those who rose to the top of society were 'encouraged by the general culture to believe that they fully deserved all they had' (Young 1994, p. vxi). But eradicating inequalities at the systemic level only to accentuate them at the individual level was also the reason that Young believed meritocracy was doomed to fail. Indeed, as he put it, meritocracy's winners, who were encouraged to believe that they were fully entitled to their good fortune and status in society, would become 'ruthless … in pursuing their own advantage' because pursuing one's own advantage had become coincidental to 'the common good' (Young 1994, p. vxi). Not only that, by structuring society so transparently and singularly along meritocratic lines, society's discontents frustrated by the established system of distributive justice could easily locate the source of inequality in a way that had perhaps been harder to do in more hetero-geneous and dispersed societies. While in 'unjustly unequal' societies the enemy is harder to identify – is it systematic racism, entrenched economic inequality, sexism, homophobia, global neoliberal capitalism, and so on and so forth that is the primary problem for inequality? – in the 'justly unequal' system of meritocracy, the problem is clear: it's the meritocratic system itself. And so, as Young's story goes, in the year 2034 the populists rebel and bring meritocracy to an end. In its place, they institute an

egalitarian and classless society where all members are regarded equally –
irrespective of their merits or lack thereof (a reflection of Young's socialist
leanings).

Many commentators have since come to see Young's story as prophetic
(*The Economist* 2018). Even his own son, Toby Young (2017), a well-
known journalist and media personality, asked in a 2017 column, 'Did my
father predict the populist revolts of the last year?' While it is hard to
dispute the importance of Young's work, we argue that reading him as an
oracle for the populist revolts taking place in our own times perhaps mis-
construes the true genius of his work. Indeed, contrary to the speculation
of those like his son, Young arguably underestimated, or at least under-
emphasized, the capacity of populism to emerge from a heterogeneous or,
what we have called here, an 'unjustly unequal' society. But that is precisely what the contemporary rise of populism has been all about. As
events like Brexit, Trump's 2016 election, the continued success of populists in Europe and Latin America, and the raft of other electoral upsets
that have occurred since have clearly demonstrated, our current populist
moment has stemmed not so much from the conditions generated by a
justly unequal society as much as from the conditions produced through an
unjustly unequal one.

Why Young is important, therefore, is not because he predicted the
populist revolt that would take place in our own time – it is clear that he
did not. Rather than treating *The Rise of Meritocracy* is as a prophetic
vision, the book is best seen as an incisive indictment of what was happen-
ing in his own era. In fact, the entire story reads – or should be read – as a
scathing analysis of the meritocratic revolution that was taking shape in
his own day, during the 1950s, that was seeking to transform meritocracy
into a 'universal ideal' and Britain into a justly unequal society (Allen
2011, p. 376). Although we know, with the benefit of hindsight, that these
aspirations were never fully realized, Young had hoped to show that meritocracy would only result in more – not less – populist resentment. This
was the irony that was the true genius of Young's story: to illustrate how
society would become more susceptible to populist resentment – and
eventually revolt – the more universally meritocratic or justly unequal it
became. Whether the inequality was perceived as unjust or just did not
matter – the inequality remained, and thus always had the potential to spur
anti-elite sentiment and revolt in the name of 'the people'. Indeed, com-
menting on Young's ideas, the twentieth-century sociologist and Young's
friend, Daniel Bell (1972, p. 65) – no relation to the political philosopher,
Daniel A. Bell, whose work we have been discussing – observes of populism that '[i]t is not for fairness, but *against elitism*; its impulse is not
justice but *ressentiment*'.

The ideal of meritocracy falls foul of this logic in one of two ways. The first is that meritocracies are by their nature oligarchies, albeit just ones. That is to say, they bestow equal opportunity, levelling the playing field as much as is practically possible, but only to entrench a hierarchical power structure (Roemer 2000, p. 18). To borrow George Mavrogordatos's (1997, p. 18) words: 'meritocracy implies oligarchy at least insofar as it entrusts any selection process based on merit to "experts" (themselves selected accordingly) rather than to the citizens or their representatives'. Meritocracy is thus an ideal defined by meritocracy's insiders or winners: the meritocratic establishment set and reinforce the rules of the game that have benefited them (Tan 2008, p. 9). More so, this establishment is likely to continue to define, interpret, and defend their particular reading of what is considered as meritorious as it suits them – something we have seen illustrated in quite explicit ways in recent years in Xi-era China. Indeed, according to Robert Klitgaard (1986, p. 1), though 'ostensibly anti-elitist', a meritocracy is by its nature sustained by a core of 'self-conscious, exploitative ruling minority' who, over time, develop an 'in-group' mentality that separates a meritocratic elite from the rest. While political meritocracy can be democratized somewhat in electoral systems such as Singapore, where citizens can vote on what meritocratic attributes matter most to them, even there, as Tan (2008, p. 8) argues, the meritocratic government draws from and is thus comprised of a largely self-sustaining 'aristocracy of talent'. In short, even with a level playing field, or even when there is meritocracy before the competition begins (Roemer 2000), the endpoint will remain uneven. The winners will go on winning while the losers will continue to lose.

This is the state of affairs that the sociologist Robert Merton calls the 'Matthew Effect' – as in the Gospel of Matthew, Chapter 25 verse 29, which states that: 'For unto everyone that hath shall be given, and he shall have abundance. But from him that hath not shall be taken away even that which he hath.' According to Merton (1968, p. 3), who coined the Matthew Effect in science, what this phenomenon leads to is 'the accruing of greater increments of recognition for particular scientific contributions to scientists of considerable repute and the withholding of such recognition from scientists who have not yet made their mark'. And it is not just in science. The popular writer Malcolm Gladwell has shown more broadly in his book, *Outliers*, that even when stratification is structured using meritocratic measures, the very best outcome will still remain skewed. As he writes:

> It is those who are successful, in other words, who are most likely to be given the kinds of special opportunities that lead to further success.

It's the rich who get the biggest tax breaks. It's the best students who get the best teaching and most attention. And it's the biggest nine- and ten-year-olds who get the most coaching and practice. Success is the result of what sociologists like to call 'accumulative advantage'.

(Gladwell 2008, p. 33)

To put this differently: in an imperfect meritocratic society, factors such as inheritance, class, race, connections, gender, and age, not to mention the key social, economic, and political institutions that govern life, still play an unacknowledged role in determining who wins and who loses. But even in a perfected meritocratic society, it is still the winners who get to set and govern the rules of the game – rules that ultimately go on to benefit mostly those like themselves. Such a system might well be fairer, but that, as Bell noted, is not what ultimately populism is against. As for the thing it is against – elitism – that, unfortunately, remains alive and well – and blatant – in a meritocracy. Indeed, as Kwame Anthony Appiah (2018) put it in the *Guardian* when discussing Young's work and the myth of meritocracy:

A system of class filtered by meritocracy would, in [Young's] view, still be a system of class: it would involve a hierarchy of social respect, granting dignity to those at the top, by denying respect and self-respect to those who did not inherit the talents and the capacity for effort that, combined with proper education, would give them access to the most highly remunerated occupations.

That political meritocracies, and its advocates, can keep striving to make procedures fairer, enabling a more diverse group of individuals the opportunity to become 'winners', does not however take away from the inescapable fact that a meritocracy will always entrench a hierarchy where there are winners and losers who will sit at polar ends of the social spectrum. This is precisely why the society and politics that meritocracy produces will never be anything other than a justly unequal one. And even when it comes to the meritocratic requirement of virtue, the very measure that distinguishes Daniel A. Bell's notion of political meritocracy from Young's more brutal fictional meritocracy, it is arguably the case that serving the interests of the ruled will do no more than placate the masses. It will never truly empower them. Rather, at the most cynical reading of Bell's work, virtue merely serves as a figleaf for covering up and excus- ing the behaviour of leaders in a highly unequal system, and one in reality that is open and prone to corruption. Moreover, how virtue is frequently conceived, practiced, and assessed raises real questions as well. For example, Bell (2016, p. 104) has noted that political leaders can be considered to exhibit virtue when they are 'willing to sacrifice their own interests on behalf of the country'. Though there is no single way to demonstrate this sacrifice, he notes that '[o]ne way of showing willingness to experience harm for the sake of the public is to do volunteer work in poor and remote rural areas for long periods'. There is much to commend here, and many populists would undoubtedly agree that politicians who are willing to do time with the people, to live and work in their communities, are certainly better than the ones who are not willing to leave the relative bubbles of their capitals – appearing as 'in touch' with the impoverished citizens of rural areas has certainly played well for the likes of Thaksin Shinawatra in Thailand, Rodrigo Duterte in the Philippines, and Hugo Chávez in Venezuela. But cosmopolitan political elites who fly in and fly out, even over a period of years, can still become the subject of populist ire. As Ivan Krastav (2017) has written of the recent European populist moment, much of the reason why meritocratic elites have become so despised by populists is because they are essentially 'a mercenary elite, not unlike the way the best soccer players are traded around to the most successful clubs across the continent. Successful Dutch bankers move to London; competent German bureaucrats move to Brussels.' They go from one location and post to another. Wherever greener pastures appear they move on, forever in search of more recognition and power. Though they may do good work, for a time, their endpoint is always elsewhere. In this way, they are not of the people – even though they may have done their time with the people. The same is true of the political leaders Bell writes of. Though, as in the case of China, the meritocratic elite may be less instrumental, it is still the case that sacrificing their own interests and doing good work is often a prerequisite for promotion to higher office. Yes, experiencing harm for the sake of the public may produce benefits to the public – just as acquiring a star football player from abroad will likely boost a team's competitiveness, to refer back to Krastev's analogy. But they are no more of the people, or from that community, as international superstars are of the teams they are hired to play for. Having done their time, and paid their dues, political elites move on. And this, to return to Krastav (2017), is what populists detest most. 'People trust their leaders not only because of their competence but also because of their courage and commitment, and because they believe their leaders will remain with their own in times of crisis rather than being helicoptered to the emergency exit', Krastav (2017) writes.

> Paradoxically, it is the convertible competencies of the present elites, the fact that they are equally fit to run a bank in Bulgaria or in Bangladesh or to teach in Athens or Tokyo, that make people so

suspicious of them. People fear that in times of trouble, the merito-
crats will opt to leave instead of sharing the cost of staying.

(Krastev 2017)

An aspiring political leader who uses his or her time in the provinces as
mere training or as a public relations ploy for a better, higher political
posting in the capitals therefore further entrenches the chasm separating
the leaders from the led – even when the intentions are 'virtuous'.

And so, no matter how virtuous, socially-inclined, and intelligent the
ruling elite are, this meritocratic oligarchy will still likely breed popular
ressentiment, which is the second way that meritocracy falls foul of the
populist logic. Though the bulk of the people's resentment in a justly
unjust social order will necessarily have to be self-directed – given their
lot is the direct result of their own lack of intelligence and virtue – it can
also manifest as a rebuke of the systemic inequality and associated sense
of disempowerment by which society is structured. When these sentiments
coexist, as they invariably do, Sandel (2018, p. 356) argues, 'they make
for a volatile brew of anger and resentment against elites that fuels populist protest'. In this way, meritocracies in fact face the same potential risks
of populism that democracies do. Though theoretically structured to give
all people a voice and the potential to hold positions of power, regardless
of one's creed or class, democracies are almost always hierarchical and
exclusionary, entrenching power and breeding resentment among the
powerless. Even the best representative democracies invariably engrain a
fundamental division between those who govern and those who are governed over time. This is because, to quote Alex Goerlach and Dawn Nakagawa (2016): 'Chief among the flaws of representative democracy is that
out of the many, few can be chosen to represent the people. This inherent
exclusivity makes the chosen few form – whether they wish to or not – a
class of their own' – a situation that is reflected in everyday talk about 'the
political class', a much (and perhaps increasingly) maligned grouping that
is perceived as inward-looking, self-referential, careerist, out-of-touch
from 'the real world' (Allen and Cairney 2015; Allen 2018). Even the
most virtuous or socially-minded political representative can, over time,
lose touch with those they represent – indeed, the time and travel demands
on political representatives in large-scale democracies almost make this an
inescapable situation, with such politicians often having little actual
contact with the constituencies that they purport to represent. Added to this
is the nature of contemporary party politics itself, whereby loyalty, rather
than merit, tends to be what gets noticed and rewarded. As Goerlach and
Nakagawa continue: 'The party system also compromises meritocracy.
Within the party system it is loyalty to the party that is most highly

rewarded, at the expense of other considerations, such as competence.'
What all this adds up to is yet another factor why citizens can become so
distrusting and resentful of the elite political class – those who are selected
to run for office are often party loyalists from a relatively narrow social
stratum and career path, rather than people from the wider spectrum of
society. Similarly, in a meritocracy only a small, select elite will ever
qualify for leadership despite the system's promise that, for those who
work hard enough and demonstrate a willingness to serve the public's
interests, greater opportunities will present themselves to you. But this is
only the theory. What we have seen in practice is that, over time, the elite
class will ossify and 'the fluidity and dynamism unleashed by meritocracy'
will be 'replaced by a rigid caste system' that will lead to 'widespread discontent' (Young 2017). Though all this may be notionally just, what even-
tuates is almost never equal.

Young's story aptly demonstrates the potential for mass populist resentment *against* meritocracy when meritocracy becomes a universal ideal.
But it leaves two important issues unresolved with respect to our analysis
of political meritocracy and populism. The first is the unclear distinction
between economic and political meritocracy in Young's story. This is an
oversight that Bell (2016, p. 239) highlights when distinguishing why his
observations about political meritocracy are less likely to succumb to the
same fate as Young's. Indeed, there is an important difference here
between Young's and Bell's notion of meritocracy. Whereas Young's
meritocratic society primarily emphasizes intellect, as we have discussed,
Bell argues that a political meritocracy must elevate virtue above all other
merits. If Young's ends up being more of a technocratic meritocracy (as
virtue is of little importance in his story), Bell's argument is that society
should be ruled by the virtuous first and foremost. When this is the case,
theoretically speaking, it should diminish the likelihood that meritocracy's
so-called winners become arrogant and solipsistic. Though inequalities
will still be produced by such a meritocracy, they will be easier to stomach
for the masses than the inequalities generated from a more economic form
of meritocracy, which is prone to what Thomas Piketty (cited in Pearce
2014) calls 'meritocratic extremism'.

Such an argument – if virtue is actually valued – is fair. Switching intellect with virtue will at least diminish the reasons for mass populist resentment and revolt against the ruling elite, and will aim to keep leaders 'in
touch' with the people as opposed to technocrats' cold remove and distance from them in the name of objectivity. This was the apparent outcome
of the PAP's efforts to become more 'compassionate' in their meritocratic
governance. But even so, an important and underlying source of resentment remains: a meritocracy that emphasizes virtue first and intellect last

will do nothing to equalize the *structural* inequalities where a minority is chosen – by the minority they will join – to sit above the majority. Just think: in Bell's account of meritocratic China, the endpoint is to draw from the masses a small group of individuals with above average virtue, social skills, and intellect who are then granted the power to govern the majority. If Bell the sociologist is correct, then political meritocracy's apparent justice (or virtue) will not redress one of populism's core grievances, which is inequality.

Second, Young's story cannot account for the rise of populist leaders *within* meritocracies. Empirically, as we have cited throughout this book, we see clear examples of politicians selected and promoted via meritocratic processes employ populist tactics in order to secure popular support. Yet in a perfect world, there should be no cause for politicians to employ populist tactics to win power and govern in properly functioning meritocracies – the most virtuous and meritorious should simply rise through the 'fair' system, without the need to play popularity politics and appeal to the people versus the elite. This therefore presents its own interesting puzzle, which would require further detailed analysis. Here, we can only briefly identify what we suspect is the key reason for this conundrum.

Young's meritocratic society is one where the principles and practices of meritocracy have become universalized – that is to say, his fictional society is governed transparently and singularly along meritocratic lines. In that society, meritocracy is the only governing ideology. Along with eradicating the need for ambition, competition, and flexibility, the system has also eradicated any need for society's winners to justify their privilege or appease the discontent of society's losers. In practice, no society would ever work this way, not even when meritocracy has been elevated to the status of official governing ideology. Bell (2013, p. 17) has made this point: a '[p]ure meritocracy' or 'a political order in which the constitution vests ultimate sovereignty in a ruling group solely on the grounds that that group has relevant competence and virtue ... is hard to imagine today'. This is the same point Ansgar Allen (2011, p. 376) noted in highlighting the difference between Young's meritocracy and the meritocratic practices actually seen in present-day UK. In the absence of a pure meritocratic political system, politicians have to compete with each other for popular support. This is not only the case in democracies, where this is obviously necessary, but in competitive authoritarian contexts as well, where although the electoral landscape may be severely unfair and uneven, elections still play a role in bestowing legitimacy on incumbents (Levitsky and Way 2010).

According to Wenfang Tang (2016, p. 157), even truly authoritarian regimes today spend a great deal more time 'maintaining political power by responding to public demand' than by threatening the use of force. Not having to compete in multiparty elections does not mean there are no pressures to adequately represent and appease majority interests. In this regard, playing the populist card (even if sparingly) can be an effective means of securing mass allegiance, or at least tampering down dissent in a nonviolent manner. For Tang (2016, pp. 8–9), this is why the CPC leadership has revived the Mass Line ideology, a populist practice evocative of Mao's rule that seeks to consult with and gather the ideas and concerns of the masses and iteratively implement them with the CPC policy framework – but practically has meant in the Xi era making public displays of the punishment of corrupt CPC officials to appease public demands around 'cleaning up' the party (Tiezzi 2013). All told, Tang contends, the CPC's 'ability to maintain this Populist Authoritarian culture is one reason' for its continued legitimacy and sustainability (Tang 2016, p. 160). Given that no political system today is purely meritocratic, it thus leaves the door open for political leaders to exploit populist strategies to supplement their meritocratic attributes in securing power. In short, it does not seem that one can fully escape populism, even in a meritocracy.

4 Conclusion

In the face of the surge of populist success not only in the 'usual' settings of Europe and the Americas – regions with long-established histories of populism – but also in the less-expected sites of Africa and the Asia-Pacific region, there has been a scramble to consider not only the 'how's' and 'why's' of the populist revival, but also the question of 'what can be done?' Beyond discussions of how liberal democracies can implement particular reforms to challenge or curtail populism, several commentators' eyes have drifted away from the liberal-democratic paradigm, and towards the East, considering how completely different political systems might be able to provide an example of how to avoid the populist threat in the first place. Yet claims about the ability of these systems to withstand populism have not been seriously analysed in an in-depth way. In this light, this book opened with the important question: are political meritocracies (such as China and Singapore) immune to the threat of populism?

As it has shown, the answer is both yes and no. There are numerous empirical examples of populism in countries that hew closest to the political meritocratic ideal: in China, Bo Xilai's New Left-inspired populism, the revival of the *San Nong*, the CCP's re-embrace of the Mass Line ideology, and Xi Jinping's adoption of certain populist tropes are all evidence that the country is far from 'populism-proof', while in Singapore, populist undercurrents and rising anti-elite tension offer seeds of resistance against the PAP's near-uniform dominance of the city-state's political life, and have forced the PAP to change their approach. To posit political meritocracy – or at least those countries that hew closest to its ideal in the contemporary political landscape – as immune to populism is thus evidently false, and overplays the actual meritocratic system in place in such countries.

At the same time, it is also important to acknowledge that populism has certainly had less political purchase and success in political meritocracies than liberal-democratic systems, where numerous populist parties have not only enjoyed political success, but become part of the political 'mainstream' in several countries across the world, and where populist movements have played an important role in shifting public opinion against the ruling elite. To some extent, the reason for this lack of success in political meritocracies is obvious: populist parties that challenge the status quo are simply unable to emerge in one-party states like China, and the PAP's stranglehold on Singaporean politics de facto stops such populist parties from achieving significant and lasting political success. The cards are simply stacked against political opponents, populist or otherwise. However, as we have argued, populist *parties* are not the only manifestation of the phenomenon that matters – the populist style can be adopted by populist leaders or movements as well, and this more flexible understanding of the phenomenon allows us to make sense of populism's emergence in settings that are otherwise inhospitable to challenges to the ruling party. There are thus 'cracks in the system' for populism to emerge even in such contexts. The first, as we have outlined, is in intra-party politics, which has certainly been the case in China, where populism has been utilized by leaders as mode of negotiating power-plays *within* the CCP. The second is in the form of social movements: while populist movements in the traditional sense of public gatherings of dissent do not stand a great chance in systems that either outlaw or violently crack down on such events and protests, the proliferation of online spaces to vent anti-elite, pro-people sentiment in the Chinese and Singaporean digital communication environment has led some scholars to speak of an emerging 'digital populism' (Tai 2015) in such countries. Even in the face of China's increasingly sophisticated surveillance state and its 'Great Firewall', dissidents have found ways to voice populist sentiment online by using technology and encryption to stay one step ahead of their censors (Banjo and Chen 2019; Skoric *et al.* 2016).

Yet these significant challenges to what we might see as populism emerging in the 'traditional' sense are arguably less a result of China and Singapore's political meritocratic aspirations, and more so of the reality of their one-party (or de facto one party) regimes. So what does political meritocracy *itself* have up its sleeve when it comes to acting as a bulwark against populism? As we showed in Chapters 2 and 3, drawing on the work of Daniel A. Bell, as compared to the usual 'other' alternative to liberal democracy offered as a 'solution' to populism, technocracy, political meritocracy privileges virtue, and social skills – in that order – above intellect, whereas technocracy merely hinges on the latter attribute, elevating 'experts' to the highest office with no concern about how or why they relate to their political subjects. The centrality of virtue and sociability, and thus at least the gesturing towards the whims, feelings, and wishes of the people as the ultimate arbiters of political life should at least stem *some* of the populist demand compared to the outright and blatant elitism of technocratic politics. Technocracy, in this regard, is in many ways the clear-cut opposite of populism, whereas political meritocracy finds itself somewhere in-between the two. More so, a political meritocratic system should ostensibly stop populist leaders who lean heavily on the non-virtuous aspects of their political persona – those who truly push the 'bad manners' envelope such as Donald Trump, Rodrigo Duterte, or Jair Bolsonaro – from even being considered for positions of leadership, as their clear breaches of the rules of decorum and decency would automatically take them out of the running for such positions. Lastly, the merit-based nature of the system should theoretically provide a more just playing field in terms of citizens being able to reach positions of power: while succeeding in both technocracy and late-capitalist liberal democracy relies on the unfairly distributed privileges of birth, class, networks, and elite education, political meritocracy should pave the way for a smoother and fairer path of upward political mobility due its more fulsome conceptualization of what merit is. This should entail the idea that entering the elite is something anyone can do given hard work and virtuous striving, and thus theoretically temper the populist claim of the cards being stacked against the little people.

Of course, as we have shown, the reality of the situation does not meet the ideal: corruption is rife in China, and its political meritocracy is severely undercut as a result. A rural peasant farmer, no matter their striving or merit, is not going to reach the high echelons of CCP leadership. The system is closed to vast sectors of the populations of China and Singapore. 'Actually existing' political meritocracies simply are not as effective or promising as defenders of the system may argue. One of the lines of arguments put forward by such defenders in response to such charges is that political meritocratic systems as currently practiced are simply *not meritocratic enough* – they need to become closer to their ideal, and if political meritocracy was 'fully' implemented, populism would not have any place in such systems. Yet against such arguments, we have claimed that the more established and universal the system of political meritocracy, the more it opens the door to populism. Drawing on the work of Young in Chapter 3, we have shown that a 'full' political meritocracy, in its move towards a 'justly unequal', as opposed to 'unjust unequal' society, creates an oligarchy, accentuates failures as one's own fault, and breeds resentment for those who have done well in the system. In such a system, there would be no pressure-release valve for such resentment and anger, and thus even the merest whiff of corruption or sense that the system is rigged could set off a populist revolt.

As such, what this book ultimately demonstrates is that we need to think seriously about the solutions offered in the name of 'defeating' populism, given that the medicine prescribed to 'cure' populism can potentially be worse than what it purports to fix, and can unleash a series of other significant problems (also see Tormey 2018). More so, such solutions may not even be that effective, and in the long run can ultimately work to fan the flames of populism – a situation we have discussed in-depth in this book, and more widely, that is increasingly evident in the seeming inefficacy of many of the tactics utilized by anti-populists in Western Europe and the United States (Moffitt 2018; Stavrakakis and Katsambekis 2019). In a context where the much-hyped 'populist threat' is purported to be the greatest challenge faced by liberal democracy in decades, it of course makes sense to consider alternatives and ways to challenge or resist populism – such as political meritocracy. However, we should be equally critical and careful in our analysis of such alternatives, lest we fall into new, more problematic traps in the long run.

References

Achen, Christopher H. and Larry M. Bartels. 2016. *Democracy for Realists: Why Elections Do Not Produce Responsive Government*. Princeton: Princeton University Press.

Albertazzi, Daniele and Duncan McDonnell. 2008. 'Introduction: The Sceptre and the Spectre'. In *Twenty-First Century Populism: The Spectre of Western European Democracy*, ed. Daniele Albertazzi and Duncan McDonnell. Basingstoke & New York: Palgrave Macmillan.

Allen, Ansgar. 2011. 'Michael Young's The Rise of the Meritocracy: A Philosophical Critique'. *British Journal of Educational Studies* 59(4): 367–382.

Allen, Peter. 2018. *The Political Class: Why It Matters Who Our Politicians Are*. Oxford: Oxford University Press.

Allen, Peter and Paul Cairney. 2015. 'What Do We Mean When We Talk about the "Political Class"?' *Political Studies Review* 15(1): 18–27.

Anshu, Shi, Francois Laschapelle, and Matthew Galway. 2018. 'The Recasting of Chinese Socialism: The Chinese New Left Since 2000'. *China Information* 32(1): 139–159.

Aslanidis, Paris. 2016a. 'Populist Social Movements of the Great Recession'. *Mobilization: An International Quarterly* 21(3): 301–321.

Aslanidis, Paris. 2016b. 'Is Populism an Ideology? A Refutation and a New Perspective'. *Political Studies* 64(IS): 88–104.

Appiah, Kwame Anthony. 2018. 'The myth of meritocracy: who really gets what they deserve?' *Guardian* 19 October. www.theguardian.com/news/2018/oct/19/the-myth-of-meritocracy-who-really-gets-what-they-deserve.

Austin, J.L. 1975. *How to Do Things with Words*. Cambridge: Harvard University Press.

Au Youg, Jeremy. 2016. 'Singapore not immune to divisive, populist politics seen in the US'. *Straits Times* 2 April. www.straitstimes.com/world/united-states/singapore-not-immune-to-divisive-populist-politics-seen-in-the-us-pm-lee.

Babones, Salvatore. 2017. 'Xi Jinping: Communist China's First Populist President'. *Forbes* 20 October. www.forbes.com/sites/salvatorebabones/2017/10/20/populism-chinese-style-xi-jinping-cements-his-status-as-chinas-first-populist-president/#1db00b21152e.

Banjo, Shelly and Lulu Yilun Chen. 2019. 'Digital Dissidents Are Fighting China's Censorship Machine'. *Bloomberg Businessweek* 4 June. www.bloomberg.com/news/articles/2019-06-03/digital-dissidents-are-fighting-china-s-censorship-machine

Barr, Robert R. 2009. 'Populists, Outsiders and Anti-Establishment Politics'. *Party Politics* 15(1): 29–48.

Barr, Michael. 2016. 'Ordinary Singapore: The Decline of Singapore Exceptionalism'. *Journal of Contemporary Asia* 46(1): 1–17.

Bell, Daniel. 1972. 'On Meritocracy and Equality'. *The Public Interest* 29: 29–68.

Bell, Daniel A. 2013. 'Introduction'. In *The East Asian Challenge to Democracy: Political Meritocracy in Comparative Perspective*, ed. Daniel A. Bell and Chenyang Li. New York: Cambridge University Press.

Bell, Daniel A. 2015. 'Chinese Democracy Isn't Inevitable'. *The Atlantic* 29 May. www.theatlantic.com/international/archive/2015/05/chinese-democracy-isnt-inevitable/394325/.

Bell, Daniel A. 2016. *The China Model: Political Meritocracy and the Limits of Democracy*. Princeton: Princeton University Press.

Bell, Daniel A. 2017a. 'Assessing China's Political System: A Response to Comments'. *Philosophy and Public Issues* 7(1): 145–166.

Bell, Daniel A. 2017b. '别迷信西方民主，贤能政治是理想政治模式'. *The Thinker Studio* 23 March. https://freewechat.com/a/MzI0NjczMDIwOA==/2247483862/1?raw.

Bell, Daniel A. 2017c. 'Can Democracies Learn from China's Meritocratic System?' *Current History* 116(793): 315–319.

Bell, Daniel A. 2018a. 'Vertical Democratic Meritocracy in China: Response to Comments'. *Journal of Chinese Humanities* 4(1): 111–123.

Bell, Daniel A. 2018b. 'Towards Democracy and Meritocracy in China: A Response to Critics'. *Politics and Religion* 11(4): 899–907.

Bell, Daniel A. and Chengyang Li. 2013. 'Compassionate Meritocracy'. *Project Syndicate* 9 October. www.project-syndicate.org/commentary/daniel-a-bell-and-chenyang-lithe-rise-of-political-meritocracy-in-asia?barrier=accessreg.

Bellows, Thomas. 2009. 'Meritocracy and the Singaporean Political System'. *Asian Journal of Political Science* 17(1): 24–44.

Bickerton, Christopher and Carlo Invernizzi Accetti. 2017. 'Populism and technocracy: opposites or complements?' *Critical Review of International Social and Political Philosophy* 20 (2):186–206.

Bonikowski, Bart and Noam Gidron. 2016a. 'Multiple Traditions in Populism Research: Toward a Theoretical Synthesis'. *American Political Science Association – Comparative Politics Newsletter* 26: 7–14.

Bonikowski, Bart and Noam Gidron. 2016b. 'The Populist Style in American Politics: Presidential Campaign Discourse, 1952–1996'. *Social Forces* 94(4): 1593–1621.

Brennan, Jason. 2016. *Against Democracy*. Princeton: Princeton University Press.

Brooks, David. 2016. 'The Governing Cancer of Our Time'. *New York Times* 26 February. www.nytimes.com/2016/02/26/opinion/the-governing-cancer-of-our-time.html.

Buckley, Chris. 2017. 'Maoists for Trump? In China, Fans Admire His Nationalist Views'. *New York Times* 3 April. www.nytimes.com/2017/04/03/world/asia/maoists-for-trump-in-china-fans-admire-his-nationalist-views.html.

Burns, John and Wang Xiaoqi. 2010. 'Civil Service Reform in China: Impacts on Civil Servants' Behaviour'. *The China Quarterly* 201: 58–78.

Buruma, Ian. 2018. 'Why Is Japan Populist Free?' *Project Syndicate* 10 January. www.project-syndicate.org/commentary/japan-no-populism-reasons-by-ian-buruma-2018-01?barrier=accesspaylog.

Butler, Judith. 1990. *Gender Trouble*. New York: Routledge.

Cabestan, Jean-Pierre. 2012. 'Is Xi Jinping the Reformist Leader China Needs?' *China Perspectives*. 2012(3): 69–76.

Cambridge Dictionary. 2017. 'Cambridge Dictionary's Word of the Year 2017'. *About words: A blog from Cambridge Dictionary* 29 November. https://dictionaryblog.cambridge.org/2017/11/29/cambridge-dictionarys-word-of-the-year-2017

Canovan, Margaret. 1999. 'Trust the People! Populism and the Two Faces of Democracy'. *Political Studies* 47(1): 2–16.

Caramani, Danielle. 2017. 'Will vs. Reason: The Populist and Technocratic Forms of Political Representation and Their Critique to Party Government'. *American Political Science Review* 111(1): 54–67.

Chan, Hon S. 2010. 'Envisioning Public Administration as a Scholarly Field in 2020: The Quest for Meritocracy in the Chinese Bureaucracy'. *Public Administration Review* 7(1): S302–303.

Chan, Stephen. 2015. 'China is Neither a Civilizational State nor a Meritocracy'. *International Policy Digest* 8 June. https://intpolicydigest.org/2015/06/08/china-is-neither-a-civilizational-state-and-nor-a-meritocracy/.

Chandran, Nyshka. 2017. 'China's homegrown populism to test Xi Jinping'. *CNBC* 1 January. www.cnbc.com/2016/12/30/chinas-homegrown-populism-to-test-xi-jinping.html.

China Daily. 2018. 'Philosopher's Guide'. *China Daily* 5 February. www.china.org.cn/arts/2018-02/05/content_50416429_2.htm.

Chou, Mark. 2013. *Theorising Democide: Why and How Democracies Fail*. Basingstoke: Palgrave.

Chou, Mark. 2014. *Democracy Against Itself: Sustaining an Unsustainable Idea*. Edinburgh: Edinburgh University Press.

Chou, Mark. 2017. 'Combatting Voter Ignorance: A Vertical Model of Epistocratic Voting'. *Policy Studies* 38(6): 589–603.

Chou, Mark. 2018. 'China's Political Meritocracy Under Xi Jinping'. *The Philosophical Salon* 19 March. https://thephilosophicalsalon.com/chinas-political-meritocracy-under-xi-jinping/.

Chu, T.T. 1957. 'Chinese Class Structure and Ideology'. In *Chinese Thought and Institutions*, ed. J.K. Fairbank. Chicago: Chicago University Press.

Curato, Nicole. 2017. 'Flirting with Authoritarian Fantasies? Rodrigo Duterte and the New Terms of Philippine Populism'. *Journal of Contemporary Asia* 47(1): 142–153.

De Cleen, Benjamin. 2017. 'Populism and Nationalism'. In *The Oxford Handbook of Populism*, ed. Cristobal Rovira Kaltwasser, Paul Taggart, Paulina Ochoa Espejo, and Pierre Ostiguy. Oxford: Oxford University Press.

De la Torre, Carlos. 2013. 'Technocratic Populism in Ecuador'. *Journal of Democracy* 24(3): 33–46.

Eatwell, Roger. 2017. 'Populism and Fascism'. In *The Oxford Handbook of Populism*, eds. Cristobal Rovira Kaltwasser, Paul Taggart, Paulina Ochoa Espejo, and Pierre Ostiguy. Oxford: Oxford University Press.

The Economist. 2011. 'The princelings are coming'. *The Economist* 23 June. www.economist.com/node/18832046.

The Economist. 2015. 'Unnatural Aristocrats'. *The Economist* 3 September 2015. www.economist.com/news/china/21663273-china-and-its-role-model-singapore-meritocratic-leaders-are-under-scrutiny-unnatural.

The Economist. 2018. 'The Merits of Revisiting Michael Young'. *The Economist* 10 February. www.economist.com/news/britain/21736524-book-published-60-years-ago-predicted-most-tensions-tearing-contemporary-britain.

Fewsmith, Joseph. 2013. 'Xi Jinping's Fast Start'. *China Leadership Monitor* 41: 1–7.

Finchelstein, Federico. 2014. *The Ideological Origins of the Dirty War: Fascism, Populism, and Dictatorship in Twentieth Century Argentina*. Oxford: Oxford University Press.

Finchelstein, Federico. 2017. *From Fascism to Populism in History*. Oakland: University of California Press.

Fish, Eric. 2015. 'Has China Discovered a Better Political System Than Democracy?' *The Atlantic* 28 October. www.theatlantic.com/international/archive/2015/10/china-politics-communism-democracy/412663/.

Flinders, Matthew. 2012. *In Defence of Politics*. Oxford: Oxford University Press.

Frank, Robert H. 2016. *Success and Luck: Good Fortune and the Myth of Meritocracy*. Princeton: Princeton University Press.

Freeden, Michael. 1996. *Ideologies and Political Theory: A Conceptual Approach*. Oxford: Oxford University Press.

Freeden, Michael. 2003. *Ideology: A Very Short Introduction*. Oxford: Oxford University Press.

Freeden, M. 2017. 'After the Brexit referendum: revisiting populism as an ideology'. *Journal of Political Ideologies* 22(1): 1–11.

Galston, William A. 2018a. *Anti-Pluralism: The Populist Threat to Liberal Democracy*. New Haven: Yale University Press.

Galston, William A. 2018b. 'The Populist Challenge to Liberal Democracy'. *Journal of Democracy* 29(2): 5–19.

Gardels, Nathan. 2013. 'Intelligent Governance for the 21st Century'. *New Perspectives Quarterly* 30(1): 7-15.

Garton Ash, Timothy. 2015. 'Is the China Model Better Than Democracy?' *Foreign Policy* 19 October. http://foreignpolicy.com/2015/10/19/china-democracy-theory-communist-party-politics-model/.

Gerbaudo, Paolo. 2017. *The Mask and the Flag: Populism, Citizenism and Global Protest*. London: Hurst.

Gladwell, Malcolm. 2008. *Outliers: The Story of Success.* New York: Black Bay Books.

Goerlach, Alex and Dawn Nakagawa. 2016. 'Populism in Western Democracy: Why Now?' *Berggruen Ideas* 29 February. http://berggruen.org/ideas/populism-in-western-democracy-why-now.

Haenle, Paul and Thomas Carothers. 2018. 'The Rise of Populism and Implications for China'. *Carnegie-Tsinghua Center for Global Policy* 24 April. https://carnegietsinghua.org/2018/04/24/rise-of-populism-and-implications-for-china-pub-76162.

Han, Kirsten. 2017. 'Singapore Can Have Meritocracy or Aristocracy, But Not Both'. *Foreign Policy* 28 June. http://foreignpolicy.com/2017/06/28/singapore-can-have-meritocracy-or-nepotism-but-not-both/.

Hawkins, Kirk A. 2010. *Venezuela's Chavismo and Populism in Comparative Perspective.* New York: Cambridge University Press.

He, Baogang. 2016. 'What Exactly Is "The Chinese Ideal"'. *Perspectives on Politics* 14(1): 147–161.

He, Li. 2009. 'China's New Left'. *East Asian Policy* 1(1): 30–37.

He, Li. 2015. *Political Thought and China's Transformation: Ideas Shaping Reform in Post-Mao China.* London: Palgrave Macmillan.

Hendrie, Doug. 2015. 'In Praise of Technocracy: Why Australia Must Imitate Singapore'. *Meanjin* 74(3): 172–174.

Hernandez, Javier C. 2018. 'For Xi Jinping, Being a Man of the People Means Looking the Part'. *New York Times* 28 September. www.nytimes.com/2018/09/28/world/asia/xi-jinping-china-propaganda.html.

Ho, Benjamin Tze Ern. 2018. 'Power and Populism: What the Singapore Model Means for the Chinese Dream'. *The China Quarterly* 236: 968–987.

Ho, Kwon Ping. 2015. 'Singapore: The Next Fifty Years'. *IPS-Nathan Lectures, National University of Singapore.* 9 April. www.smu.edu.sg/sites/default/files/smu/about_smu/pdf/IPS-Nathan-Lectures_Lecture-V-Society-and-Identity-speech_090415.pdf.

Holbig, Heike and Bruce Gilley. 2010. 'Reclaiming Legitimacy in China'. *Politics & Policy* 38(3): 395–422.

Hui, Li and Lance Gore. 2017. 'Merit-Based Patronage: Careers Incentives of Local Leading Cadres in China'. *Lee Kuan Yew School of Public Policy Research Paper No. 17–03.* https://ssrn.com/abstract=2942026.

Huxley, Tim. 2016. 'Dealing with xenophobic nationalism: Lessons from Singapore'. *Lowy Interpreter* 9 December. www.lowyinstitute.org/the-interpreter/dealing-xenophobic-nationalism-lessons-singapore.

Ionescu, Ghita and Ernest Gellner (eds) 1969. *Populism: Its Meanings and National Characteristics.* London: Weidenfeld and Nicolson.

Ivarsflaten, Elisabeth. 2008. 'What Unites Right-Wing Populists in Western Europe?' *Comparative Political Studies* 41(1): 3–23.

Jacobs, Andrew and Chris Buckley. 2015. 'Move Over Mao: Beloved "Papa Xi" Awes China'. *New York Times* 7 March. www.nytimes.com/2015/03/08/world/move-over-mao-beloved-papa-xi-awes-china.html.

Jansen, Robert S. 2011. 'Populist Mobilization: A New Theoretical Approach to Populism'. *Sociological Theory* 29(2): 75–96.

Jansen, Robert S. 2017. *Revolutionizing Repertoires: The Rise of Populist Mobilization in Peru.* Chicago: University of Chicago Press.

Keane, John. 2009. *The Life and Death of Democracy.* London: Basic Books.

Kenny, Paul D. 2017. *Populism and Patronage: Why Populists Win Elections in India, Asia, and Beyond.* Oxford: Oxford University Press.

Kim, Chang-Hee and Yong-Beom Choi. 2017. 'How Meritocracy is Defined Today? Contemporary Aspects of Meritocracy'. *Economics & Sociology* 10(1): 112–121.

Klitgaard, Robert E. 1986. *Elitism and Meritocracy in Developing Countries: Selection for Higher Education.* Baltimore: Johns Hopkins University Press.

Krastev, Ivan. 2017. 'The Rise and Fall of European Meritocracy'. *New York Times* 17 January. www.nytimes.com/2017/01/17/opinion/the-rise-and-fall-of-european-meritocracy.html.

Laclau, Ernesto. 1977. *Politics and Ideology in Marxist Theory.* London: NLB.

Laclau, Ernesto. 2000. 'Foreword'. In *Discourse Theory and Political Analysis: Identities, Hegemonies and Social Change*, ed. David Howarth, Aletta Norval, and Yannis Stavrakakis. Manchester & New York: Manchester University Press.

Laclau, Ernesto. 2005. *On Populist Reason.* London: Verso.

Levitsky, Steven and Lucan A. Way. 2010. *Competitive Authoritarianism: Hybrid Regimes after the Cold War.* Cambridge: Cambridge University Press.

Levitsky, Steven and Daniel Ziblatt. 2018. *How Democracies Die.* New York: Crown.

Li, Cheng, 2017. 'Status of China's women leaders on the eve 19th Party Congress'. *China-US Focus* 30 March. www.chinausfocus.com/political-social-development/status-of-chinas-women-leaders-on-the-eve-of-19th-party-congress.

Li, Eric. 2011. 'China's Opposition: Redder than the Communist Party Itself'. *Christian Science Monitor* 30 August. www.csmonitor.com/Commentary/Global-Viewpoint/2011/0830/China-s-opposition-redder-than-the-Communist-Party-itself.

Lipsey, David. 2014. 'The Meretriciousness of Meritocracy'. *The Political Quarterly* 85(1): 37–42.

Lister, Ruth. 2006. 'Ladder of Opportunity or Engine of Inequality'. *The Political Quarterly* 77(s1): 232–236.

Liu, Ye. 2016. *Higher Education, Meritocracy and Inequality in China.* Singapore: Springer.

Mahbubani, Kishore. 2016. 'Why Asia Doesn't Have a Donald Trump or Bernie Sanders'. *New Perspectives Quarterly* 33(2): 26–28.

Mair, Peter. 2013. *Ruling the Void: The Hollowing of Western Democracy.* London & New York: Verso.

Matijasevich, David. 2018. 'Populist Hangover: Lessons from Southeast Asia'. *Asian Journal of Comparative Politics* (OnlineFirst).

Mauzy, Diane and R.S. Milne. 2002. *Singapore Politics Under the People's Action Party.* London: Taylor & Francis.

Mavrogordatos, George. 1997. 'From Traditional Clientelism to Machine Politics: The Impact of PASOK Populism in Greece'. *South European Society and Politics* 2(3): 1–26.

Mbete, Sithembile. 2015. 'The Economic Freedom Fighters – South Africa's turn towards populism?' *Journal of African Elections* 14(1): 35–59.

Mellen, Ruby. 2017. 'Anti-Corruption Populists Tend to be More Corrupt, Report Says'. *Foreign Policy* 25 January. http://foreignpolicy.com/2017/01/25/anti-corruption-populists-tend-to-be-more-corrupt-report-says/.

Merton, Robert K. 1968. 'The Matthew Effect in Science'. *Science* 159(3810): 56–63.

Moffitt, Benjamin. 2015. 'How to Perform Crisis: A Model for Understanding the Key Role of Crisis in Contemporary Populism'. *Government and Opposition* 50(2): 189–217.

Moffitt, Benjamin. 2016. *The Global Rise of Populism: Performance, Political Style, and Representation.* Palo Alto: Stanford University Press.

Moffitt, Benjamin. 2018. 'The Populism/Anti-Populism Divide in Western Europe'. *Democratic Theory* 5(2): 1–16.

Mounk, Yascha. 2018. *The People vs. Democracy: Why Our Freedom Is in Danger and How to Save It.* Cambridge, MA: Harvard University Press.

Mudde, Cas. 2004. 'The Populist Zeitgeist'. *Government and Opposition* 39(4): 541–563.

Mudde, Cas. 2007. *Populist Radical Right Parties in Europe.* Cambridge: Cambridge University Press.

Mudde, Cas and Cristobal Rovira Kaltwasser (eds). 2012. *Populism in Europe and the Americas: Threat or Corrective for Democracy?* Cambridge: Cambridge University Press.

Mudde, Cas and Cristobal Rovira Kaltwasser. 2017. *Populism: A Very Short Introduction.* Oxford: Oxford University Press.

Müller, Jan-Werner. 2016. *What is Populism?* Philadelphia: University of Pennsylvania Press.

Nadiri, Khalid. 2007. 'China's Peasant Populism: A Look Inland'. *SAIS Review of International Affairs* 27(1): 125–126.

Nathan, Andrew. 2015. 'Beijing Bull: The Bogus China Model'. *The National Interest* 22 October. http://nationalinterest.org/feature/beijing-bull-the-bogus-china-model-14107.

Nichols, Tom. 2017. *The Death of Expertise: The Campaign Against Established Knowledge and Why It Matters.* New York: Oxford University Press.

Norris, Pippa and Ronald Inglehart. 2019. *Cultural Backlash: Trump, Brexit, and Authoritarian-Populism.* Cambridge: Cambridge University Press.

Ong, Elvin. 2013. 'Populism in not a bad word'. *The Independent* 17 September. http://theindependent.sg/populism-is-not-a-bad-word/.

Ortmann, Stephen and Mark R. Thompson. 2014. 'China's Obsession with Singapore: Learning Authoritarian Modernity'. *The Pacific Review* 27(3): 433–455.

Ortmann, Stephen and Mark R. Thompson. 2016. 'China and the "Singapore Model" '. *Journal of Democracy* 27(1): 39–48.

Osnos, Evan. 2015. 'Born Red'. *The New Yorker* 6 April www.newyorker.com/magazine/2015/04/06/born-red.

Ostiguy, Pierre. 2017. 'Populism: A Socio-Cultural Approach'. In *The Oxford Handbook of Populism*, ed. Cristobal Rovira Kaltwasser, Paul Taggart, Paulina Ochoa Espejo, and Pierre Ostiguy. Oxford: Oxford University Press.

Panizza, Francisco (ed.) 2005. *Populism and the Mirror of Democracy.* London & New York: Verso.

Pappas, Takis S. 2019. *Populism and Liberal Democracy: A Comparative and Theoretical Analysis.* Oxford: Oxford University Press.

Pearce, Nick. 2014. 'Thomas Piketty: A Modern French Revolutionary'. *New Statesman*, 3 April. www.newstatesman.com/2014/03/french-revolutionary.

Perry, Elizabeth. 2015. 'The Populist Dream of Chinese Democracy'. *The Journal of Asian Studies* 74(4): 903–915.

Plato (trans. Lee, Desmond). 2007. *The Republic.* London: Penguin.

Pocha, Jehangir. 2005. 'China's New Left'. *New Perspectives Quarterly* 22(2): 25–31.

Prabhala, Achal. 2013. 'Justly Unequal: The Unlikely History of Our Greatest Delusion'. *The Caravan: A Journal of Politics & Culture* 1 March. www.caravanmagazine.in/perspectives/justly-unequal.

Prakash, Pravin. 2014. 'Understanding Meritocracy'. *Today* 25 June. www.todayonline.com/singapore/understanding-meritocracy.

Reich, Simon. 2016. 'Western populism, eastern leadership: Brexit, Trump and the rise of populism in response to globalisation'. *Asia & the Pacific Policy Society Policy Forum* 30 June. www.policyforum.net/western-populism-eastern-leadership/.

Resnick, Danielle. 2014. *Urban Poverty and Party Populism in African Democracies.* New York: Cambridge University Press.

Richburg, Keith B. and Andrew Higgins. 2012. 'Bo Xilai's ouster seen as victory for Chinese reformers'. *Washington Post* 15 March. www.washingtonpost.com/world/asia_pacific/bo-xilai-fired-in-communist-party-leadership-shakeup/2012/03/15/gIQA3uaLDS_story.html?utm_term=.900aadbe4332.

Roberts, Kenneth M. 1995. 'Neoliberalism and the Transformation of Populism in Latin America: The Peruvian Case'. *World Politics* 48(1): 82–116.

Roberts, Kenneth M. 2003. 'Social Correlates of Party System Demise and Populist Resurgence in Venezuela'. *Latin American Politics and Society* 45(3): 35–57.

Roberts, Kenneth M. 2015 'Populism, Political Mobilizations, and Crises of Political Representation'. In *The Promise and Perils of Populism: Global Perspectives*, ed. Carlos de la Torre. Lexington: The University Press of Kentucky.

Roemer, John E. 2000. *Equality of Opportunity.* Cambridge: Harvard University Press.

Rooduijn, Matthijs. 2014. 'The Nucleus of Populism: In Search of the Lowest Common Denominator'. *Government and Opposition* 49(4): 573–599.

Rummens, Stefan. 2017. 'Populism as a Threat to Liberal Democracy'. In *The Oxford Handbook of Populism*, ed. Cristobal Rovira Kaltwasser, Paul Taggart, Paulina Ochoa Espejo, and Pierre Ostiguy. Oxford: Oxford University Press.

Sandel, Michael. 2017. 'Lessons from the Populist Revolt'. *Project Syndicate* 4 January. www.project-syndicate.org/onpoint/lessons-from-the-populist-revolt-by-michael-sandel-2017-01?barrier=accesspaylog.

Sandel, Michael. 2018. 'Populism, Liberalism, and Democracy'. *Philosophy & Social Criticism* 44(4): 353–359.

Saunders, Peter. 2006. 'Meritocracy and Popular Legitimacy'. *The Political Quarterly* 77(s1): 183–194.

Saward, Michael. 2015. 'Agency, Design and "Slow Democracy"'. *Time & Society* 26(3): 362–383.

Shin, Doh Chull. 2013. 'How East Asians View Meritocracy: A Confucian Perspective'. In *The East Asian Challenge to Democracy: Political Meritocracy in Comparative Perspective*, ed. Daniel A. Bell and Chenyang Li. New York: Cambridge University Press.

Shirk, Susan L. 2018. 'The Return to Personalistic Rule'. *Journal of Democracy* 29(2): 22–36.

Skoric, Marko, M., Qinfeng Zhu, and Natalie Pang. 2016. 'Social media, political expression, and participation in Confucian Asia'. *Chinese Journal of Communication* 9(4): 331–347.

Somin, Ilya. 2013. *Democracy and Political Ignorance: Why Smaller Government is Smarter*. Palo Alto: Stanford University Press.

Stanley, Ben. 2008. 'The Thin Ideology of Populism'. *Journal of Political Ideologies* 13(1): 95–110.

Stavrakakis, Yannis and Giorgos Katsambekis. 2014. 'Left-wing populism in the European periphery: the case of SYRIZA'. *Journal of Political Ideologies* 19(2): 119–142.

Stavrakakis, Yannis and Giorgos Katsambekis. 2019. 'The populism/anti-populism frontier and its mediation in crisis-ridden Greece: from discursive divide to emerging cleavage?' *European Political Science* 18(1): 37–52.

Stavrakakis, Yannis, Giorgos Katsambekis, Alexandros Kioupkiolis, Nikos Nikisianis, and Thomas Siomos. 2018. 'Populism, Anti-Populism and Crisis'. *Contemporary Political Theory* 17(1): 4–27.

Stewart, Devin and Jeffrey Wasserstrom. 2016. 'The Global Populist Surge Is More than Just a Western Story – Just Look at Asia'. *The Diplomat* 10 December. https://thediplomat.com/2016/12/the-global-populist-surge-is-more-than-just-a-western-story-just-look-at-asia/.

Taggart, Paul. 2000. *Populism.* Birmingham: Open University Press.

Taggart, Paul. 2004. 'Populism and Representative Politics in Contemporary Europe'. *Journal of Political Ideologies* 9(3): 269–288.

Tai, Zixue. 2015. 'Networked Resistance: Digital Populism, Online Activism, and Mass Dissent in China'. *Popular Communication* 13(2): 120–131.

Tan, Kenneth Paul. 2008. 'Meritocracy and Elitism in a Global City: Ideological Shifts in Singapore'. *International Political Science Review* 29(1): 7–27.

Tan, Kenneth Paul. 2013. 'Meritocracy and Political Liberalization in Singapore'. In *The East Asian Challenge to Democracy: Political Meritocracy in Comparative Perspective*, ed. Daniel A. Bell and Chenyang Li. New York: Cambridge University Press.

Tan, Kenneth Paul. 2016. 'How Singapore is fixing its meritocracy'. *Washington Post* 16 April. www.washingtonpost.com/news/in-theory/wp/2016/04/16/how-singapore-is-fixing-its-meritocracy/?utm_term=.466a9ff34de3.

Tan, Kenneth Paul. 2017. 'Resisting Authoritarian Populism: Lessons From/For Singapore'. *Foreign Affairs* 15 May. www.foreignaffairs.com/sponsored/resisting-authoritarian-populism-lessons-fromfor-singapore.

Tang, Wenfang. 2016. *Populist Authoritarianism: Chinese Political Culture and Regime Sustainability*. Oxford: Oxford University Press.

Tiezza, Shannon. 2013. 'The Mass Line Campaign in the 21st Century'. *The Diplomat.* 27 December. https://thediplomat.com/2013/12/the-mass-line-campaign-in-the-21st-century.

Tormey, Simon. 2018. 'Populism: Democracy's *Pharmakon?*' *Policy Studies* (OnlineFirst): 1–15.

Townsend, James R. 1977. 'Chinese Populism and the Legacy of Mao Tse-Tung'. *Asian Survey* 17(11): 1003–1015.

Urbinati, Nadia. 2017. 'Populism and the Majority Principle'. In *The Oxford Handbook of Populism*, ed. Cristobal Rovira Kaltwasser, Paul Taggart, Paulina Ochoa Espejo, and Pierre Ostiguy. Oxford: Oxford University Press.

Vogel, Ezra. 1989. 'A Little Dragon Tamed'. In *Management of Success: The Moulding of Modern Singapore*, ed. Kernial Singh Sandhu and Paul Wheatley. Singapore: Institute of Southeast Asian Studies.

Wembridge, Mark. 2015. 'Singapore ponders populist future after PAP victory'. *The Financial Times* 14 September. www.ft.com/content/1f81be7a-5a8a-11e5-9846-de406ccb37f2.

Weyland, Kurt. 2001. 'Clarifying a Contested Concept: Populism in the Study of Latin American Politics'. *Comparative Politics* 34(1): 1–22.

Weyland, Kurt. 2003. 'Neopopulism and Neoliberalism in Latin America: How Much Affinity?' *Third World Quarterly* 24(6): 1095–1115.

Weyland, Kurt. 2017. 'Populism: A Political-Strategic Approach'. In *The Oxford Handbook of Populism*, ed. Cristobal Rovira Kaltwasser, Paul Taggart, Paulina Ochoa Espejo, and Pierre Ostiguy. Oxford: Oxford University Press

Wiles, Peter. 1969. 'A Syndrome, not a Doctrine: Some Elementary Theses on Populism'. In *Populism: Its Meanings and National Characteristics*, ed. Ghita Ionescu and Ernest Gellner. London: Weidenfeld and Nicolson.

Wodak, Ruth. 2015. *The Politics of Fear: What Right-Wing Populist Discourses Mean.* London: SAGE.

Wolff, Jonathan. 2006. *An Introduction to Political Philosophy*. Cambridge: Hackett Publishing.

Womack, Brantly. 2017. 'Xi Jinping and Continuing Political Reform in China'. *Journal of Chinese Political Science* 22(3): 393–406.

Wong, Kevin. 2018. 'Social Skills in *The China Model*: An Amendment to Daniel Bell's "Menu" of Leadership Qualities'. *Politics and Religion* 11(4): 891–895.

Wong, Benjamin and Xunming Huang. 2010. 'Politics Legitimacy in Singapore'. *Politics and Policy* 38(3): 523–543.

Xu, Ben. 2001. 'Chinese Populist Nationalism: Its Intellectual Politics and Moral Dilemma'. *Representations* 76(1): 120–140.

Yeo, George. 2017. 'Civilizational States Like China Are Less Prone to Populism'. *Huffington Post* 24 May. www.huffpost.com/entry/china-populism-unlikely_b_5915d90ee4b0031e737d45aa.

Young, Michael. 1958. *The Rise of Meritocracy*. New Jersey: Transaction Publishers.

Young, Michael. 1994. 'Introduction to the Transaction Edition'. In *The Rise of Meritocracy*, Michael Young. New Jersey: Transaction Publishers.

Young, Toby. 2017. 'Did my father predict the populist revolts of the last year?' *The Spectator* 8 April. www.spectator.co.uk/2017/04/did-my-father-predict-the-populist-revolts-of-the-last-year/.

Yu, Haiyang. 2014. 'Glorious Memories of Imperial China and the Rise of Chinese Populist Nationalism'. *Journal of Contemporary China* 23(90): 1174–1187.

Yu, Jie. 2019. 'Party versus Market: Xi Fails to Resolve China's Contradictions'. *Chatham House* 16 March. www.chathamhouse.org/expert/comment/party-versus-market-xi-fails-resolve-chinas-contradictions.

Zeng, Jinghan. 2013. 'What Matters Most in Selecting Top Chinese Leaders? A Qualitative Comparative Analysis'. *Journal of Chinese Political Science* 18(3): 223–239.

Zhang, Taisu. 2016. 'China's Coming Ideological Wars'. *Foreign Policy* 1 March. http://foreignpolicy.com/2016/03/01/chinas-coming-ideological-wars-new-left-confucius-mao-xi/.

Zhang, Weiwei. 2012. 'Meritocracy Versus Democracy'. *New York Times* 9 November. www.nytimes.com/2012/11/10/opinion/meritocracy-versus-democracy.html.

Zhang, Yongle. 2018. 'The Future of Meritocracy: A Discussion of Daniel Bell's *The China Model*'. *Journal of Chinese Humanities* 4(1): 49–64.

Zhang, Zhibin. 2015. 'Crowding Out Meritocracy? – Cultural Constraints in Chinese Public Human Resource Management'. *Australian Journal of Public Administration* 74(3): 270–282.

Index

For Product Safety Concerns and Information please contact our EU
representative GPSR@taylorandfrancis.com
Taylor & Francis Verlag GmbH, Kaufingerstraße 24, 80331 München, Germany

www.ingramcontent.com/pod-product-compliance
Lightning Source LLC
Chambersburg PA
CBHW050540270326
41926CB00015B/3323

* 9 7 8 1 0 3 2 2 3 9 0 8 8 *